Our Guerrero Family

Pictorials & Captions

Tata Jobo Elizes
Publisher, 2010

Our Guerrero Family
Tatay Jobo Elizes
2010

Copyright

ISBN-13: 978-1453842904
ISBN-10: 145384290X

Publisher
Tatay Jobo Elizes
June 2010

Pictorials & Captions

Rev. Dr. Eugenio & Filomena Guerrero
(My grandparents on my mother side)

**Taken in 1940 in Manila, Grandpa Genio at 52 and
Gramma Filo at age 42**

**Rev. Dr. Eugenio Tanyag Guerrero, 1888 - 1945
Mrs. Filomena Jamito Diaz-Guerrero, 1898 - 1985**

Pictorials & Captions

About the Author and the Book

I created & published this book of pictures and stories to honor my grandparents on my mother side.

My name is **Jobo Guerrero Elizes,** the 2nd oldest grand child in the Guerrero Family of Talisay, Camarines Norte. The whole clan is described in pictures and stories in this book, starting from our grandparents, and then my parents, then their siblings, then my brothers and sisters, then my cousins, our descendants, and extended families through relatives and various affinities. I was born in 1934 in Manila but grew up partly in Camarines Norte during the Japanese time in the 1940s.

My mother, **Esther Guerrero,** was the oldest child of the Guereros. The Guerreros are 10 children in all, and is quite a large family, as each one generated his or her clan, which form part of the Guerrero kindred. My biography is not of utmost important here. Suffice it to say that I created this book to document and describe in pictures and in little stories my various relatives in this family. Pictures convey thousand words. I am presenting them all here to convey stories via descriptive captions, names, places, events and occasions. Another purpose of this book is to relate the history of our family in order that the young generation will be able to trace their roots and family beginnings, otherwise there will be no other way to know their roots, relations, lineage, origins, names, birthdays, locations, professions, careers, phones and interesting aspects of their lives. I included also extended families who are related to my grandfather and grandmother on my mother side. My Elizes kin on my father side belongs to another book.

Dedication

I heartily dedicate this book to all members of the Guerrero Family and to all extended families and to all future generation of the bloodline of Guerrero.

Acknowledgement

I wish to acknowledge and express my gratitude to all those who contributed in the making of this book, specially all the families who have given me their pictures and individuals who posed for me. One theme or part in this book depicted the 1989 family reunion in New York state, which was the largest gathering of our Guerrero Clan. I give due credit and thank my aunt, **Norma D. Guerrero,** who spearheaded and managed this grand reunion. She lent me most of the photographs of the reunion, including past photographs of the member-families. It took me months of painstaking labor to produce this in regular book format, in paperback. Now, this book is easily available for purchase online.

Table of Contents

Part 1: Great-Grandparents

The parents of Grandmother Filomena are: **FLORENTINO CHAVEZ DIAZ (Tata Tinong), and RUPERTA BARILLA JAMITO (Nana or Nana Mintang).**

1913 Picture: Wedding Pictures of Eugenio & Filomena Guerrero
with their parents

Top Pic: Nana Mintang, age 35 + Tata Tinong, age 39 (great grandparents)
Bottom Pic: Grandma Filomena, age 15+ Nana Mintang+ Tata Tinong+ Tatay Genio, 26.

Pictorials & Captions

Great-Grandparent's Story.

Our great granfather, Florentino, or Tata Tinong, and his **older brother Juanso Diaz** plus another **cousin Domingo Diaz** were not from Camarines Norte. They originated from Surigao province in Mindanao. Legend tells us that they were cattle merchants, engaged in trading cattles or cows, and traveling to many provinces for this purpose. They visited and conducted their cattle business in Talisay, where there were cattle farms and ranches during those times. These three Diaz brothers and cousin most likely overstayed in Talisay and were probably enamoured by the beauty of the place, the goodness of the inhabitants and lovely maidens and by the good business prospects.

Our great-grandmother, **Ruperta, or Nana Mintang,** belonged to the Jamito clan of Talisay, one of the biggest families in the town. The Jamitos probably owned ranches and herds of cows and conducted business with visitors and traders. The Diaz brothers were strangers in town of Talisay and considered "estrangero" or foreign traders. In the course of these visits and stays in Talisay by the Diaz brothers, it is highly possible that Tata Tinong became attracted to Nana Mintang and the courtship began.

My oldest uncle, **Eler Guerrero,** happened to travel to Surigao during the 1970s, as part of his duties as Treasurer of the United Church of Christ in the Philippines, or UCCP. He met there a certain Judge Diaz and they exchanged pleasantries and talked about the Diaz family name. Uncle Eler noted that the physical apearance of Judge Diaz has some resemblance with our own Diaz ancestors, but the genealogical line was not easy to trace. Uncle Eler also found out that the Diaz family in Surigao was into cattle business, which was a good coincidence.

Eventually, **Tata Ansoy and Tata Tinong,** the early Diaz brothers who came to Talisay as cattle traders, married local ladies. In the case of our great-grandfather Tata Tinong, he married our great-grandmother, **Ruperta Jamito** around 1895. They settled down in

Talisay and raised nine children.

Epidemic killed the children, except Filomena.

According to our grandmother **Nanay Filo,** she was the oldest out of nine children in their family. Her brother, **Juan,** was 2nd child. Grandmom was named Filomena at birth, and was known as Pilo or Nana Pilo to many in Talisay. She had other brothers and sisters, named **Agustin, Isidro, Icasiano, Maria, Rosario and 2 others.** The other names are difficult to recall because all of them died during the severe epidemic that struck the town of Talisay, except **daughter Filomena,** who survived the tragic event. Many children of other families died in Talisay. Her brother Juan, age 11, was the last one to die. The young children died within three to four months period. Filomena was just 12 years old at the time. Tata Tinong and Nana Mintang were totaly devastated by the tragedy. They were terribly disillusioned and disheartened. The tragedy drove Tata Tinong to gamble away most of their real properties and their herds of cattle. Legend says that their family had substantial landholdings in Talisay because of the ranch and cattle, plus their coconut plantation and ricelands. The coconut and rice farms, reduced by land reform, still exist until now, which I visited in 2010.

Grandma Filo used to narrate how she enjoyed going out into the family farm with her father to see the farm in barrio Sta. Cruz and the rice fields near the highways, specially during rice planting season. She also loved looking at the herds of cattle with "Diaz" trademark stamped on each cow, while her dad counted them. Tata would say to her, "Someday all these will be yours." Filomena always thought her dad was a very proud man, until he realized the reality of tragedy resulting from the untimely deaths of all his children, except one. He decided to get away from Talisay to try to forget the catasthropy and left his wife and one child and drown his misery elsewhere. He must have sold a lot of property because he traveled to foreign lands. It was said that he went around Asia, and touched China, Singapore, and Malaysia along the way. Such expensive travels would have been enough to reduce assets and resources of the family.

Left Photo, 1920s: Grandfather Tata Tinong Diaz. He died in 1936, at age 64.
Right Phto, 1953: Grandmother Nana Mintang Jamito Diaz. She outlived Tata as she died much later in 1964, at age 86

Circa 1953: Grandma or Nanay Filomena + Great-Grandma Nana Mintang

After a year of traveling, Tata returned home thinking that the remaining child Filomena was also gone but much to his surprise he found her alive and healthy. She had survived the epidemic. To celebrate Tata's joy in seeing Filomena alive, he gave a big party inviting the whole townspeople of Talisay.

Filomena as solo daughter or "unica hija"

When life returned to normal to Tata Tinong and Nana Mintang, they found themselves without children to attend to and therefore they could live carefree lives and so much free time in their lives just busy accumulating wealth from their farms and business. Legend says that Nana Mintang became addicted to "Entrequatro" a form of card game popular among th elderly in Talisay. I guess Tata Tinong too had plenty of time to play other forms of gambling. The care for their only child was entrusted to the maids. I think this was the time when their wealth started to deplete. In later life, Nana Mintang maintained a stall at the Talisay public market until Japanese time.

Tata Tinong died in 1936 of pulmonary tuberculosis at the age of 64, while Nana Mintang died in 1964 at age of 86. There was no specific illness given to Nana's death but she was suspected to have had early cancer of the mouth, maybe due to constant chewing of beetle nuts (nga-nga) a practice of the old people. Chewing beetle nuts irritates the lining of the mouth and sometimes cause cancer.

My paternal grandparents on the Guerrero side.

The parents of **my frandfather, Eugenio Guerrero,** were **GREGORIO GUERRERO** and **AQUILINA (Inang) TANYAG**.

They were not from Bicol. **Great-Grandpa Gregorio Guerrer**o was from San Pedro, Laguna, while **Great-Grandma Aquilina**, which we called **Inang**, was from the town of Taguig, Rizal, formerly

Morong Province. They raised their children in San Pedro, more particularly, in the barrios of Cuyab and San Antonio, where there were many Guerreros. It seems that my my grandfather, **EUGENIO,** called TATAY, was their eldest. Their second child was **GERONIMO**, called LOLO EMONG by us. The third was a girl, named **GRACIANA**, that we called LOLA GRACIA, who lived in Muntinglupa. We have very little information about our paternal great-grandparents, because of distance. They lived in Laguna while we lived in Camarines Norte.

1915 Picture: Great-Grandmother **Aquilina (Inang) Tanyag Guerrero.**
This is most precious picture, her only one archived.
Unfortunately, there's no picture of
Great-**Grandfather Gregorio Guerrero.**

Grandfather Eugenio visited Laguna often, due to his field trips as a pastor and continuing education in Manila for advancement in his religious studies. Near the end part of this book, I will relate more info about our **Lolo Emong (GERONIMO GUERRERO),** younger brother of Lolo Genio (EUGENIO GUERRRERO, our grandfather) as Emong married a lady from Bicol also and they stayed in Bicol for a while.

Part 2 - Grandma - Filomena Guerrero

My Grand-Mother, Filomena Jamito-Diaz Guerrero, was born in July 5, 1898, to Ruperta Jamito and Florentino Diaz. We call her, Nanay, a Filipino way of identifying the "First Lady" in any Filipino family. It is term of endearment for the most important and beloved person. All mothers of this world are the best people on earth.

Top Left: 1960s, Nanay Filomena Vda.de Guerrero. . .**Top Right:** 1953: Norma & Nana. **Rest of the picures** show Nana and Nanay (mother and daughter).

Grandma or Nanay Filomena was the first child in the family of nine children. Early on and being the oldest child, she learned the responsibility of caring for her brothers and sisters. Being the first girl to be born in the family, she ssumed the role of second mother. The story goes that during her growing years, she already had assumed the responsibility of supervising the care of her younger siblings while her own mother was working on some important task for the family welfare. Although she was left to supervise the maids and the servants to do the actual work, she was also expected to give direction to all household concerns. At the time the children were growing, a bad epidemic devastated evey towns, and eight (8) of her brothers and sisters died, succumbing to the epidemic over a three-month period.

Circa 1910 - Young women's basketball team

As I narrated earlier, her father (Tata Tinong) became desperate and left town. He traveld as fas as he can go and started selling off his lands and properties. When he finally came back from his extensive travel, he found out that Filomena had blossomed into a pretty young maiden and was the object of worship of many young boys from the towns of Talisay and Daet.

She had also turned into a star basketball player and was captain of the women's team. She was the most sought after of among the young women.

Circa 1910 - Young Filomena

Filomena at one point was trained as "maestra", or teacher and as such she was called "Maestrang Filo." She was not a spoiled child, even if she was the ramaining survivor among nine children during that tragic epidemic. As she learned many chores early in life, she was the one who spoiled her parents. Her parents, Tata and Nana, were the ones enjoying life of the rich. That's why as a young lady and still in her teens, she was prepared to assume a married life. She actually married at age 15 only.

Part 3: Grandpa - Rev. Dr. Eugenio Tanyag Guerrero And Family

Our **GUERRERO CLAN** started with the wedding of **EUGENIO TANYAG GUERRERO,** our esteemed grandfather, to **FILOMENA JAMITO DIAZ,** our beloved grandmother. Their wedding was held in 1913. Below is their wedding picture.

Pictorials & Captions

Rev. Dr. Eugenio and Mrs. Filomena Guerrero

We call our grandfather, TATAY, and our grandmother, NANAY. Tatay was born in San Pedro, Laguna, in September 9, 1888, Nanay was born in Talisay, Camarines Norte in July 5, 1898. Please note that Tatay was 25 and Nanay was only 15 years old when they got married. A difference of ten years. It was a union of a Tagalog gentleman to a Bicolana lady. Tatay was a Protestant while Nanay was a Catholic. To top it all Tatay was in fact a Pastor or Minister of the Protestant faith.

At left is 1920s pic of Rev. Dr. Eugenio T. Guerrero, newly ordained Doctor of Divinity from Union Theological Seminary. He died early in 1945, at age 56.
At right is 1960s pic of Nanay Filomena Guerrero, who outlived her husband by many years, when she passed away in 1985 at age 86.

Despite the difference in age, in ethnic origins, and in religious faiths, their union was one beautiful and successful marriage that lasted many years, that resulted in 12 children and produced several generations of Guerreros since then as I write this book in this early part of the 21st century. Families are not immuned to untimely deaths as two children died in infancy. Tatay Genio, our grandfather, died in 1945 at age 56, after 32 years of marriage. Nanay dedicated her life and took care of the whole family for many more years.

Brief Biography of Eugenio Guerrero Sr

Tatay graduated from the **Union Theological Seminary** in Manila, **now** under the Philippine Christian Unversity of Manila and located in Dasmarinas, Cavite. As a young man of about 20, he finished Bachelor's degree in Theology. This was aproximately 1908, during the early period of American influence and protestant evangelization campaign.

Philippines was basically a catholic country and Tatay, being bright and hungry for education was probably attracted by scholarship in theology. He served his church in his hometown after being ordained as a young pastor immediately after graduation. He must have served there in San Pedro Evangelical Church for about 3 years. His name still appears today as number 3 in the roster of Pastors that served in that church. Then he accepted assignment by the Presbyterian Missions to go to Bicol. He bacame pastor in Daet, capital of Camarines Norte. He converted the local people, specially young people to his fold. His classmate, **Pastor Vicente Navarette** was assigned to Naga, Camarines Sur. Their leader was the **American Pastor, Rev. Stephen Smith,** who supervised the whole Bicol region.

I think on or about 1925, Tatay decided to further his theological studies, after having been a pastor for almost 20 years since graduation with bachelor's degree.

Pictorials & Captions

1925 Picture: L-R: Rev. Dr. Eugenio Guerrero + Dr. Enrique Sobrepena + Dr. Vicente Navarette. Union Theoloical Seminary in Manila.

He pursued and earned his Doctor of Divinity degree, and probably defended his thesis successfully. He was one of the three original graduates who earned the doctorate degree. **The other two prominent graduates were Dr. Enrique Sobrepena, who became Bishop of the United Church of Christ in the Philippines, called UCCP, and Pastor Vicente Navarette, Pastor in Camarines Sur.** The Bachelor's degree in Theology was earlier earned while hey were young. The picture below shows my father as a new graduate in Theology from the same school of Union Theological Seminary in Manila.

Circa 1908: My father Eugenio Guerrero is shown in far right
with his two classmates.

Love Story of Eugenio & Filomena

This is the love story of Tatay and Nanay. Tatay held protestant
services on Sundays and established a weekly fellowship among
the young people and teenagers after the service. It was in those
meetings that he spotted and took special attention to a young
lass. The young lady was Nanay, age 14 or 15. Nanay was raised
as a Catholic and only on few occasions did she go with friends to
the fellowship meetings. Because Tatay was much older by about
ten years, she spurned his attention and lessened her attendance
in the weekly meetings. This, however, did not discouraged Tatay.
This time he decided to work his way by courting her parents.

Mom was the only child left of nine children of Nana Mintang and Tata Tinong. She was the only one who survived the deadly epidemic in Talisay.   Her parents therefore gave her all the attention and privileges that she desired short of spoiling her. Since she always got her way, Nanay did many foolish things to discourage Tatay's early proposals.   Tatay diverted his attention and sought the help of her parents and other town elders to help advance his cause. Tatay was quite successful. The rest is history. They married in June 1913, Tatay at age 25, and Nanay at age 15.

They told us that the marriage in the beginning was a difficult one due to the disparity in their ages and background. Nanay was very young, coming from a well-off family, was a little bit spoiled, but not inherently, but was due to the fact that she became one and only child after the deaths of her siblings. Nanay married Tatay, who was a college graduate, more knowledgeable due to his higher learning, and more specially so as a minister of the church, and probably more reserved and formal in his ways. Nanay, on the other hand barely finished high school, but sports-minded, was a member of the girls basketball team, and more athletic. While she lacked education, she was however trained and became "Teacher Filomena" or "Maestrang Pilo", which are commendable traits. But in the long run, they surmounted these differences in their marriage. Tatay was a patient man. Nanay narrated that it took five months for her to realize that she was already married and had to become a dutiful wife to her husband. Good thing that Tatay waited until she mellowed down from her being a difficult young wife at the beginning.

Shown below are pictures of the young family that grew into much bigger family and the children into adulthood.

Top Left: 1915: Nanay Filomena + Tatay Eugenio + Baby Esther (their first baby, my mom).

Top Right:1918: Baby Elisa (2nd child), age 2+ Baby Eler (3rd), age 1+ Baby Esther (1st), age 4

Below Left: 1930: L-R: Naomi, age 11+ Eler, 13+ Ser, 4+ Arte, 2+ Eliza, 9+ Esther, 16

Below Right: 1926: L-R: **Front:** Naomi, 6+ Ser, 1+ Eliza, 5+. . . **Middle:** Tatay+ Nanay+. . .**Back Row:** Eler, 8 + Esther, 12

Complete Family Pic

1961 Pic: Manila: The first generation Guerreros, showing grandmother (Nanay) + my aunts and uncles. Picture was taken in 1961. Three insets are superimposed, those of my grandfather (Tatay), my mom Esther and Aunt Norma.

Front, Squatting: (1) Vencer, 1938-1958

Middle Row, L-R: (1) Gene, 1934 + (2) Eler, 1918-1991 + (3) Nanay Filomena Vda de Guerrero, 1898-1985 + (4) Arte, 1928-2004 + (5) Ser, 1926-2000

Back Row, L-R: (1) **Inset**, Tatay/Pastor Genio Guerrero, 1888-1945 + (2) **Inset**, Esther, 1914-1945 + (3) Lulex, 1937 + (4) Naomi, 1920-2001 + (5) Eliza, 1922 + (6) **Inset,** Norma, 1930

Note: Norma (inset only) could not be in the picture as she was in USA. Tatay & Esther (insets only) passed away in 1945.

Part 4
Mom Esther & Lolo Genio Deaths

Tragic events, like untimely deaths, happen in families, whih are sometimes unavoidable. We can only recall them with great understanding. In 1945, during the liberation of the Philippines from Japanese rule, Esther's family was staying in Vinzons, formely Indan town. She was oldest sister and the only one married with 4 children. One day, Esther developed severe infected acne at the nape of her neck. The infection developed into a severe septicemia, the presence of pathogenic bacteria in the bloodstream. There was no available medication she needed at that time, like antibiotics. Because of the unavailability of this important medication to help Esther's illness, she died so suddenly. It was totally unexpected. Her husband, Job and their 4 children were totally devastated and caught unprepared with her loss.

Grandparents Genio and Filo who lived in the next town of Talisay were notified. Grandpa Genio, upon larning of the tragic death, grieved to the maximum. He became emotinally distraught and developed massive cerebral hemorrhage and instantly died. He was 57 at that time.

Esther died at 10:30 PM in the night of July 18, 1945 and Tatay Genio followed six hours later, at 4:30 AM in the morning of July 19, 1945.

It was a very sad day, due to the two tragic deaths which occured in Guerrero family, one after the other. At that time, the older children were in college in Manila, who were Eler, Naomi and Ely. The only ones to help and console Grandmother were the younger children, Ser, the oldest left in Talisay, plus Arte, Norma, Gene, Lulex and Vencer. The death of Esther left behind a husband and four young children, Susan, the oldest at 12, Job Jr (myself), age 10, Hilda, age 6 and Bobby, age 2. My mom Esther was only 31

Pictorials & Captions

years old when she passed away. More than anybody else, Grandma was the most aggrieved due to loss of Grandfather and her oldest daughter, Esther, my mom, simultaneously. Two deaths in the family was too great a tragedy to bear.

Eugenio died young at age 56. Previous to his death, he had a stroke and was already paralyzed. He had several treatments and was on theraphy to be able to walk around and manage himself with the aid of a care giver.

Part 5 - Esther & Job Elizes Sr. Fam.

1940: Mom Esther+ Dad Job Elizes+ Susan+ JobJr+ Hilda. Bobby not born.

Elizes Family Pictures

1993 and 1996 Pics: Siblings: Susan+ Jobo+ Hilda+ Bobby

Susan & Arsenio Ferrer Family Pics

Left Pic: 1953 Wedding: Susan Elizes & Arsenio Ferrer
Right Pic: Circa 1969, Young cousins: Front l-r: (1) Chevy Elizes
(2) Marie Elizes (3) Roman Ferrer (4) Leo Ferrer. . . .
Back, l-r: (1) Tetchie Elizes (2) Mimi Hollmann
(3) Ana Grace Ferrer (4) Cynthia Ferrer

2009 Pic: Oldest Son Noel Ferrer & Family = L-R: Noel+ Wife Esther+ Son Abe+ Daughter Sarah+ Son Jay

Noel Ferrer & Family Pics

Left Pic: 2008: Noel Ferrer and Daughter Sarah
Right Pic: 2009: Son Jay Ferrer and Wife, newly wed

Brothers Noel and Marvin Ferrer Pics

Left Pic, 2010: Noel Ferrer (1st Ferrer child) & Wife, Esther
Right Pic, 2010: Marvin Ferrer (3rd Ferrer child)

Left Pic: 2000, 2nd Ferrer child (oldest daughter) Maribel Ferrer & Roly Abella
Right Pic: 2006, 4th Ferrer child, Ana Grace Ferrer Solidarios, right+
her daughter Rachel Jean, left

Circa 1990s Pic: Cynthia Ferrer (5th Ferrer Child) and Solomon Roxas Family.
Left Pic: Young Cindy Roxas+ Mom Cynthia+ Young Charli+ Dad Sol Roxas.
Right Pic: Their oldest son, Sol Jr or Chaloy

2001 Pic: Leo Ferrer (6th Ferrer child) + Wife Josie?

2000s Pic: Roman Ferrer (Youngest Ferrer Child) + Lynn Fajardo & children
Inset Pic: Kathleen + Ryan

Pictorials & Captions

2003 Pic of the Grandma Susan Ferrer and her clan in Vancouver Canada.
Front Row, L-R: Seated: (1) Roly Abella+ (2) Sol Roxas (3) Roman Ferrer (4) Roman
Wife & child (5) Ryan (6) Leo Ferrer (7) Josie Ferrer
Bck Row: L-R, Standing: (1) Luis Solidarios (2) Maribel Ferrer Abella (3) GRANMA
SUSAN ELIZES-FERRER (4) Ana Ferer Solidarios (5) Cynthia Ferrer Roxas
(6) Rachel F. Solirarios (7) Kim F. Solidarios (8) Charli F. Roxas
Middle Row, Children, L-R: (1) Leo Son Ferrer (2) Kathleen Ferrer
(3) Cindy F. Roxas (4) Susie Ferrer

More Susan Ferrer Clan Pics

2009: Rachel Jean Solidarios Wedding with Husband in LA
2009: Jay Ferrer Wedding with Wife in Manila

Luis Solidarios & Kim. . . .+ Rachel Jean+ Mom Ana+ Kim

Marvin Ferrer+ Child Adrienne. . . Ex-wife Beng+ Adrienne

**2009 Xmas Pics: Left Pic: Shown are Charli Ferrer+ Cindy Roxas + Sol Roxas +
Cornellette & Baby Monette+ Cynthia Roxas+ Chaloy Roxas. . .+
Riht Pic: Cynthia Roxas+ Ana Solidarios+ GRANDLADY SUSAN FERRER+
Maribel F. Abella**

More Susan Ferrer Clan Pics

Top Left: Christmas 2009 Party Pic
Top Right: Christmas 2009 Pic
Bottom Left: Sol and Cynthia Roxas
Bttom Right: Grandma Susan Ferrer & Kim Solidarios

Jobo and Cora Elizes Family Pics

Top Left: 1991: L-R: Bottom-Up: Cora Elizes+ Jobo Elizes+ Tetchie Elizes Bowen+ Noelle Bowen+ (back) Elizabeth Esmeralda-Elizes+ Chevy Elizes+ Baby Chad Elizes+ Vincent-Bimbo Reyes+ Baby Marjorie Reyes+ Marie Elizes-Reyes.
Top Right: 1984: Marie and Tetchie in NY
Bottom Left: 1990: Marie and Bimbo Reyes
Bottom Right: 2007: L-R: Marjo Reyes+ Bimbo Reyes+ Marie Reyes+ Marty Reyes+ Cora Elizes+ Jobo Elizes+ Marvin Reyes

----

Next Page Pictures:
Top Pic: 1999: L-R: Chad + Chevy+ Jeb+ Tetchie+ Abeth+ Cora + Jobo
Mid Left: 2006: Chad HS Graduation: L-R: Karines+ Abeth+ Chevy+ Chad
Mid Right: 2005: L-R: Noelle+ Chad+ Jeb+ Abeth+ Karines+ Tetchie
Bottom Pic: 2006: L-R: Hiden Noelle+ Jeb+ Cora+ Tetchie+ Abeth+ Chevy+ Karines+ Chad

Pictorials & Captions

Hilda Elizes and Rico Ramirez Family Pictures

Top Left: Couple Rico & Hilda Ramirez

Top Right: 2000: L-R: Jackie R. Caragan, holding Baby Jaden+ Alan Caragan+ Joy Ramirez+ Hilda Ramirez+ Federico Ramirez(Rico) + Leila R. Wong, holding Jaron+ Brent Wong

Bottom Left: 2000: L-R: Bottom-Up: Rico & Hilda Ramirez+ Leila & Brent Wong+ Alan & Jackie Caragan+ Joy Ramirez.

Bottom Middle: 2005: L-R: Kalen Caragan, 2+ Jaden Caragan, 5+ Nolan Caragan, 1+ Jaron,4+ Micah, 2.

Bottom Right: 2004: Brent and Leila Wong Family with Jaron and Micah

Bobby and Merlie Elizes Family Pictures

Top Left: Couple Merlie and Bobby Elizes

Top Right: Bobby and Merlie and children Romerl and Eszel

Bottom Left: Romerl and Evelyn Elizes and children Eric and Christina

Bottom Right: Eszel and Joe Tobias Family and children Emmelene-Jade and Jared

Part 6 - Eler & Rosa Guerrero Family

Top Left: Couple Eler and Rosing Guerrero

Top Right: 1950: Family Picture, showing Eler and Rosing Guerrero and initial children, Eleanor+ Minna+ Cynthia

Bottom Left: 1980: Eler and Rosing Guerrero in their home in Bgy. Sta Cruz, Talisay

Mid Right: 1985: L-R: Bottom-Up: Minna+ Mom Rosing+ Dad Eler+ Eleanor+ (at back) Dave+ Cynthia+ Eugene

Bottom Right: 1987: In Togas: L-R: Bottom-Up: Nanay Rosing + Tatay Eler+ (at back)+ Eleanor+ Minna+ Cynthia

Eleanor Guerrero and Abel Atienza Family Pics

Top Left: 1970s: Eleanor & Abel and 3 babies: Amar, Mimah, and Excel
Top Right: Eleanor overlooking Taal Lake

Bottom Left: 2000s: Amar and Sa-me Atienza + 3 children: Friendlander, age 11+ TheaMariz, 5+ Azel Mar, 2
Mid Right: 2000s: Jemimah (Mimah) Atienza, single + 2 pamankins

Bottom Right: 2000s: Excel and Jing Atienza family + 3 kids: Xeane-Izec, age 7 + Ethan-Jex, 3 + Exanne-Lois, 2

Minna Guerrero & Peping Magyawe Family Pics

Top Left: 1970s: Young Couple Minna an Peping Magyawe

Top Right: 2000s: L-R: John Paul Magyawe+ Johannah-Joy Magyawe+ Mom Minna Guerrero Magyawe+ Joselito-Peping Magyawe.

Bottom Left: 2000s: L-R: Joy Magyawe+ Tita Norma Guerrero+ Minna Magyawe

Bottom Right: 200os: John Paul and Joy

Minna is a nurse in NY.
Peping is a civil engineer in NY
Joy is involved in the arts and theatre in NY
John Paul is a professional in NY

Cynthia Guerrero and Ernest Sayers Family Pics

Top Pics: 2000s: Cynthia Guerrero & Ernest Sayers overlooking nice Alberta Lake

Bottom Left: 1980s: The late Ray Gaspar and Cynthia Guerrero first family+ 3 children: Daughter Sidhara+ Son Devine+ Son Love (all Gaspars).

Middle Right: 9/12/2005: Wedding: L-R: Devine-Dino Gaspar+ Mom Cynthia Guerrero-Sayers+ Groom David Duncan+ Bride Sidhara Gaspar+ Love Gaspar. Place: Edmonton, Alberta, Canada.

Bottom Right: Baby Dara Ray Duncan, born in July 7, 2006, first grandchild of Cynthia

Dave Guerrero an Mary Family Pictures

Top Left: 2008: Couple Dave and Maria Guerrero

Top Right: 1970s: Parents Eler & Rosing Guerrero and brother and sisters of Dave Guerrero: as shown left to right, from bottom-up: Minna+ Nanay Rosing+ Tatay Eler+ Eleanor+ . . .(at back) Dave+ Cynthia+ Eugene.

Bottom Left: 2000s: Dave & Maria Guerrero and 3 children.

Bottom Right: 2008: Dave Guerrero Family + Wife Maria+ 3 children, with Nanay Rosing Guerrero

Dave is Expert and Consultant in Piggery Industry
Maria is Lay Leader in the evangelical church.
Eldest daughter is finishing nursing in 2008.
The family lives in Antipolo, Rizal.

Part 7
Naomi Guerrero and Chas. Hollmann Family

Top Left: 1950s: Couple Naomi and Charles Hollmann
Top Right: 1950s: Charles Hollmann, as Gen, Manager of Manila Hotel
Bottm Left: 1960s: Young Mimi+ Young Chiqui+ Young Pinky
Bottom Right: 1980s: Mom Naomi + Her 3 Teens: Pinky+ Chiqui+ Mimi

More Hollmann Family Pictures

Top Left: 1970s: Mimi + Dad Charlie Hollmann+ Pinky + Mom Naomi Guerrero-Hollmann

Top Right: 1980s: Hula Dancers Hollmann Teen Sisters: Pinky+ Mimi+ Chiqui

Bottom Left: 1980s: Mom Naomi + her 3 teens, Pinky+ Mimi+ Chiqui

Bottom Right: 1980s: Mom Naomi + Mimi+ Pinky+ Chiqui

Chiqui Hollmann and Prandy Yulo Family Pics

Top Left: 1989: NY: Chiqui + Prandy + their 2 kids: Chino, age 5+ Chia, 3.

Top Right: 1989: NY: Young Chia and Young Chino

Bottom Left: 1998: Xmas, Manila: L-R: Prandy + Chiqui+ Chino+ Chia

Middle Right: 2004: Chia 18th Birthday: L-R: Dad Prandy+ Mom Chiqui+ Chia, age 18,+ Chino, 20

Bottom Right: 2005: Chia + Chino+ their cousin Jay jay (Mimi's youngest son)

Chia Career in Modeling

Top Left & Bottom Left: 2007 Dislay Ads showing Chia Yulo

Top Right: 2005: Chia modeled for PINK magazine, showin the trendiest summer preppy outfits, basic mach khakis and eye catching accessories.

Bottom Right: Another modeling ad of Chiaiqui

It seems Chia Yulo is following the footsteps of her famous mom Chiqui Hollmann-Yulo with career activities related to showbiz. She displays similar grace and beauty.

Charlene Adelaide (Pinky) Hollman Family Pictures

Top 3 Pics: L-R: Mom Charlene Hollmann (Pinky)+ Veronique + Chloe

Bottom Left: Chloe Cartier + Veronique Girard

Bottom 2 center Pics: Cousins Veronique+ Monique+ Chloe+ Hans

Bottom Right: 1991: Charlene Hollmann and Dominique Girard + daughter Veronique, As flower girl during wedding of Maqui & Carmelo.

Mimi Family Pictures

Top Left: 1980s: Chase Hollmann, oldest son of Mimi. He died later.

Top Right: 1975: Mimi Hollmann appeared as Cover Girl in some magazines

Bottom Left: Jay-jay Hollmann, youngest son of Mimi

Bottom Mid: 2004: Hans William Hollmann Licerio, 3rd child of Mimi

Bottom Right: 2005: Monique Hollmann Licerio, 2n child of Mimi

Part 8
Elisa (Ely) & Nonoy Yogore Family

Top Left: 1990s: Their Mom Ely & Dad Nonoy Yogore

Top Right: 1980s: Chicago: L-R: Marilyn+ Bong+ Mary Ellen+ Beth+ Mom Ely+ Eugene+ (at front) Michelle+ John

Bottom Pic: Family Portrait: 1990s: L-R: Bottom-up: Eugene+ Mom Ely+ Dad Nonoy+ Bong+ (a back) Marilyn+ Mary Ellen+ John+ Michelle+ Beth

More Yogore Pics

Top Pic: 1981: Front: L-R: Grandkids: Ana+ Kim+ Philip+ Ely+ Marita
2nd Row: L-R: MaryEllen & Ed Kimmeth+ Ely & Nonoy+ John & Tammy
3rd Row: L-R: Eugene & Leena+ Bong & Rita+ Michelle+ Marilyn & Guy Thompson+ Beth & Chester Kath
Middle Pic: 2002: Mini-reunion: Chicago: Front: Mom Ely+ Norma+ Baby Cassie+ Darby+ Dad Nonoy
Back Row: Dylan+ Marilyn+ Sidney+ Michelle+ Keegan+ Mary Ellen+ Ella+ Beth+ Monique
Botom Pic: 2006: L-R: Seated: PhilipYogore+ EllaKath+ DarbyJones+ AlexYogore+ CassieJones+ Riley-Ann+ Gage+ Morgun+ ConnorYogore. . .**Back Row:** Dylan Kimmeth+ SidneyThompson+ Kim+ Ana+ Ely+ MaritaYogore+ Keegan Thompson

More Yogore Pics

Top Left: 1980s: Family Portrait of Bong & Rita Yogore Family + children, l-r, Ana+ Marita+ Philip

Top Right: 2000s: Fam Portrait of Marilyn and Guy Thompson's + children: Keegan & Sidney

Mid Left: 1990s: Fam Portrait of Eugene Leena Yogore's + children Kim and Ely

Bottom Left: Fam Portrait pf Beth Yogore Kath and only child Ella Kath

Botom Right: Fam Portrait of Mary Ellen & Ed Kimmeth's + only son, Dylan Kimmeth

More Yogore Pics

Top Left: 1990s: Michelle Yogore Jones with daughters Cassie and Darby

Top Right: 1990s: John and Shannon Yogore with children Alex and Gage (Blond boy)

Mid Left: 1990s: John Yogore and his 5 children: Alexandra-Alex+ Gage (Blond)+ Connor+ Morgun and Riley-Ann

Mid Right: 2000s: L-R: Mom Rita+ Marita+ Grandma Ely+ Ana+ Dad Bong Yogore

Bottom Left: Cousins: Keegan Thompson+ Dylan Kimmeth+ Sidney Thompson

Bottom Right: 2004: Illinois: L-R: Seated: Nonoy Yogore+ Ely Yogoe+ Lulex Licerio+ Merlie Elizes+ . . .Back Row: Mary Ellen & Ed Kimmeth+ Ella Kath+ Beth Kath+ Guy Thompson+ Marilyn Thompson

Part 9 - Ser and Zeny Guerrero Family

Top Left: 1994: NY: Mom Zeny and Dad Ser Guerrero, during wedding of Ser Jr and Baba Eliazo

Top Right: 1970s: RP: L-R: Bttom-up: Ser Jr+ Dad Ser+ (at back) Emily + Albert+ Nina

Bottom Left: 1994: NY: Dad Ser+ Mom Zeny+ Nina + Albert

Bottom Right: 1980s: RP: L-R: Seated: Emy+ Daughter Katrina+ Albert and Nitz+ son Mark and daughter Katrina. . . . **Back Row:** Ser Jr+ Nina + Dad Ser Sr.

More Ser Pics

Top Left: 1970s: RP: L-R: Bottom-Up: Emy+ Baby Katrina+ Albert+ Baby Mark+ Nitz+ Baby Andrea+ . . .Ser Sr+ Ser Jr (both at back)

Top Right: 2000s: Sicat Family Portrait: L-R: Seattle WA: Gerry Sicat+ son Karlo+ daughter Katrina+ Emy Sicat

Mid Left: 2000s: Bong and Nina Mercado, nee Guerrero

Mid Right: 2000s: Parents Baba & Ser Jr Guerrero+ 2 kids: Sean Nicholas & Margaret Elise

Bottom Left: Their house in Tagaytay City

Bottom Mid: 2000s: Fami Portrait: Dad Albert+ Mom Nitz+ Mark+ Katrina+ Ser Albert

Bottom Right: Their house in Cavite City

Part 10 - Arte and Nene Guerrero Fam.

Top/Bottom Left: 1960s: Dad Arte and Mom Nene Guerrero

Top Right: 2000s: Fam Portrait of Arcy & Margot + L-R children: Kara Jean+ Myles+ Fiona Marie

Mid Right: 2000s: Fam Portrait of Arturo-Boy & Cindy + 4 children: L-R: Corina-Coco+ Giro+ Carmela-Chyla+ Catriona-Cayt

Bottom Rt: 2000s: Fam Portrait of Timmy & Gerogia + children: Miguel+ Francesca-Eka

More Arte Pics

Top Left: 1980s: Bottom-up: L-R: Dad Arte+ Mom Nene+ Joji+ Aya+ Margot+ Timmy+ Arturo

Top Right: 1990s: Mix Couples/Guest: L-R: Bottom-Up: Joji Acop+ Georgia Guerrero+ Aya Valerio+ Laurie Licerio (Guest)+ Cindy Guerrero+ Chiqui Yulo+ (back) Dennis Acop+ Timmy Guerrero+ Buddy Valerio+ Arturo Guerrero+ Prandy Yulo

Mid Left: 1990s: L-R: Prandy & Baby Chino & Baby Chia+ Buddy & Baby Yuri+ Dennis & Baby Jackie+ Arturo & Baby Coco

Bottom Left: 1990s: L-R: Chiqui & Babies Chino/Chia+ Aya & Baby Yuri+ Joji & Baby Jackie+ Cindy & Baby Coco

Mid/Bottom Right: 1990s: Arte/Nene Granchildren: L-R: Front-Back: Dave Acop+ Raisa Valrio+ (back)DennisJoseph Acop+ Jackie Acop+ Coco Guerrero+ Chyla Guerrero+ Giro Guerrero+ Yuri Valerio+ Chase Hollmann (Naomi's clan)

Pictorials & Captions

More Arte Pics

Top Left: 1980s: Joji Guerrero & Dennis Acop Wedding
Top Right: Acop children: L-R: Dencio+ Dave+ Jackie

Mid Right: 1990s: Budby and Aya Valerio Family + children (back) Raisa & Yuri + (front) Andrei and Stephano

Bottom Left: 1970s: Guerrero Sisters-Nurses: L-R: Margot+ Marinella-Aya+ Jocelyn-Joji

Bottom Right: 2000s: Arcy and Margot Rada Family + children Kara Jean+ Myls+ Fiona Marie (Fima)

Part 11 - Norma Diaz Guerrero

Norma Diaz Guerrero, shown below in her younger years + pictures with Nanay Filomena Vda. De Guerrero and Nana (Lola) Mintang (Ruperta Jamito-Diaz), circa 1956.

More Norma pics

Above, Norma with her pet cat, Tabbi + + + Lower Pic, Norma & Nanay Filo + + Norma with Naomi and Nanay Filo.

Part 12
Eugenio (Gene) & Piding Guerrero Fam.

2000s: Family Portraits of Gene & Piding Guerrero + 2 children: Euric an Melissa (2 other children not shown)
1990s: Top Pic: L-R: Euric+ Marifi+ Dad Gene+ Genegene+ Melissa+ Mom Piding

More Gene Family Pics

Middle Pics: Euric in toga + Wife Kristen Ward+ Melissa dancing
Bottom Pic: 2001: Genegene Graduation+ Mom and Dad Piding & Gene Guerrero

Mariefi Guerrero & Patrick James Family

Family Portraits: 2000s: Mariefi and Patrick James together with their 4 children: Oldest, John Edward (Jack)+ 2nd, Connor Patrick+ 3rd, Aidan James+ youngest, Mackenzie Rayne. They live in Connecticut.

Bottom Right: 2000s: Brothers of Mariefi: Gene-gene and Euric

Part 13
Lulex & Eduardo Licerio Family

Top Pic: 1980s: Family Portrait: Bottom-Up: L-R: Baby Monique+ Carmelo Soriano+ Maqui Soriano+ Baby Hans+ Mom Lulex+ Dad Ed Licerio+ Laurie+ Christina+ Jun
Bottom Pic: 2000s: 9 Grandchildren: L-R: Bottom-up: Lexie + Riley + Zachary+ Noah+ Baby Jackson+ Baby Evan+ Twin Sydney+ Twin Janelle + Taylor

More Licerio pics

Top Pic: 2000s: Licerio Siblings: L-R: Bottom-up: Maqui Soriano+ Christina Cruz+ Laurie Hart+ Jun Licerio

Bottom Pic: 1998 Wedding: L-R: Laurie+ Christina + Monique+ Mom Lulex+ Groom Ed-Jun+ Hans+ Dad Ed+ Maqui+ Carmelo Soriano + Ringbearers young Zachary+ Young Taylor. (Bride Judy not shown)

Jun and Judy Licerio Family

Family portraits: All Pictures show Jun and Judy Licerion with their 3 children: Young Lexie and Twins Janelle Nicole and Sydney Claire

Laurie Licerio and Eldon (TJ) Hart Family Pictures

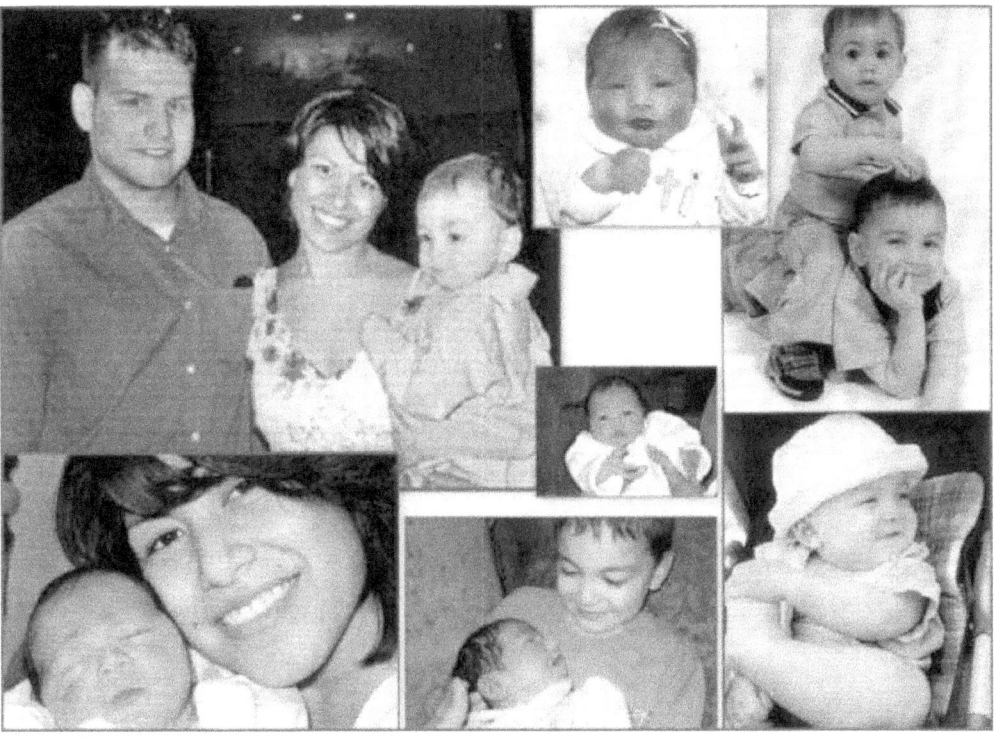

2000s Family Pictures showing Laurie and TJ Hart and their three young children: Riley, born in 2003 + Jackson Fisher, born in 2005+ Lilah Blue Hart, born in 2007. They live in Virginia Beach.

Brandon Cruz and Christina Licerio Family

Top Picture: 2000s: Family Portrait: Brandon & Christina Cruz and son Baby Evan

Bottom Pic: Solo Pic of Baby Evan Cruz

Part 14
Vencer & Violeta (Didi) Guerrero Family

Left Pic: 1960s: Mindoro: Vencer D. Guerrero, still a bachelor working in a ranch

Top Right: 1970s: Family Portrait: L-R: Young Baba+ Mom Didi+ Dad Vencer+ Young Bimbi + (at back) Young Lala + Young Thssa (Jethro not yet born)

Bottom Right: 1989: Family Portait: L-R: Vencer-Krystian(Bimbi) + Maria-Filomna (Lala) + Maria Feliza (Baba) + Mom Violeta Mision (Didi) + Jethro + Dad Vencer Guerrero+ Maria-Theresa (Thessa)

Rafaella Rae

Chloe Angelique

Danica Marie

2005: Family Portraits: Myk & Thessa Alba + triplets: Chloe, Rafaela & Danica

More Vencer Pics

Top Left: 2004: RP: L-R: Myk Alba+ Thessa Guerrero Alba+ Ricky Castro+ Lala Guerrero Castro and Son Jericho-Cocoy Castro
Top Right: Lala + Son Cocoy+ husband Ricky Castro

Mid Left: 2005: SF: L-R: Ricky Castro+ Cocoy Castro+ Lala Catro+ Baby Jazzlin
Mid Right: Rex Ribano and Baba Guerrero Ribano in Melbourne, Australia

Bottom Left: 2002, Talisay Home: L-R: Lulex Licerio+ Dave Guerrero+ Vencer-Bimbi Guerrero Jr+ Baba Guerrero+ Violeta-Didi Guerrero
Bottom Right: 2002: Talisay Home: L-R: Lulex+ Didi+ Dave+ Bmbi+ Norma+ Baba

Part 15 - Mix Photo Collection

Top Left, 1937, Daraga Albay: L-R: Front: Young Susan Elizes+ Daddy Job Elizes+ Young Jobo Elizes Jr.+ Friend1+ Friend2. . . **Back:** Esther Guerrero Elizes+ Eliza Guerrero+ Naomi Guerrero+ Nanay Filomena Diaz Guerrero.

Top Right, 1937, Daraga, Albay: L-R: Guerrero Sisters Eliza+ Esther+ Naomi

Bottom Left, 1937, Daraga, Albay: L-R: Guerrero Sisters Naomi+ Esther+ Eliza

Bottom Right, 1939, Manila: L-R: Front: Children Jobo ElizesJr+ Lulex Guerrero+ Susan (Sanie) Elizes. . . . **Back:** Naomi Guerrero+ Eler Guerrero+ Esther Guerrro-Elizes+ Tatay Genio Guerrero+ holding Baby Hilda Elizes+ Eliza Guerrero.

Mix Pictures

Top Left: ab. 1925, Rev. Dr. Eugenio T. Guerrero, Union Theological Seminary, Manila

Bottom Left: 1961, Filomena Vda. De Guerrero, Manila

Right Photo: 1941, Manila: Tatay Eugenio and Nanay Filomena Plus three children, l-r, Eliza + Eler+ Naomi.

Ten Guerrero Children Group Pictures

Top Pic, 1961, Manila: L-R, From Bottom-Up: Vencer+ Gene+ Eler + Nanay Filomena+ Arte + Ser + Tatay Eugenio, inset + Esther, inset+ Lulex+ Naomi+ Eliza+ Norma, inset. (Note: Tatay died in 1945; Esther died in 1945; Norma was in USA)

Middle Pic, 1961, Manila: L-R, Bottom-Up: (some with spouses): Gene+ Vencer+ Ser+ Eler & Rosing+ Nanay Filomena+ Nene & Arte + Norma, inset+ Nonoy & Ely Yogore +Naomi & Charles Hollmann

Bottom Pic, 1961, Manila: L-R, Bottom-Up: Lulex+ Ely+ Nanay Filomena+ Naomi+ Norma, inset+ Vencer+ Ser+ Eler+ Arte+ Gene+ Esther, inset.
Mix Pictures

More Pics - Mix

Top Left: 1947, Manila: Ely Yogore+ Baby Bong Yogore

Top Middle: 1953, Manila: Bottom-Up: Lulex+ Nanay Filo+ Norma+ Naomi

Bottom Left: 1953, Manila: Bottom-Up: Vencer+ Nanay Filo+ Norma+ Ser+ Naomi

Bottom Middle: 1961: Manila: Hilda + Bobby Elizes

Bottom Right: 1961: Manila: Young Chiqui + Young Charlene Hollmann

More Mix Pictures

Top Left: 1953, Manila: L-R: Naomi G. Hollmann+ Ely G.Yogore+ Norma Guerrero+ Lulex Guerrero

Top Right: 1953, Manila: Solo Picture of Norma Guerrero, in nurse uniform

Bottom Left: 1950s, Manila: L-R: Bottom-Up: Gene+ Lulex+ Vencer+ Arte+ Nene+ Norma+Ser+ Zeny + Norma

Bottom Right: 1950s, Manila: L-R: Gene+ Eler+ Arte + Ser

1980s Picture

1980s Picture: L-R: Botom-Up: Nanay Filomena, inset+ Eler Guerrero+ Naomi Guerrero-Hollmann+ Vencer Guerrero+ Norma Guerrero+ Arte Guerrero

Group Pictures

Bottom Pic: 1961 Reunion: L-R: Bottom-UP: Young Eugene-eler Guerrero+ Young Dave Guerrero+ Mary Ellen Yogore+ Joji Guerrero+ Lulex Guerrero+ Chiqui Hollmann+ Norma Guerrero+ Nanay Filomena+ Pinky Hollmann+ Marilyn Yogore+ Nana Mintang+ Aya Guerrero+ Nene Guerrero+ Eleanor Guerrero+ Naomi Hollmann, with Baby Mimi+ Vencer Guerrero+ Eugene Yogore+ Cora Elizes+ BabyTetchie Elizes+ Jobo Elizes+ Gene Guerrero+ Bong Yogore+ Arte Guerrero+ Minna Guerrero+ Eler Guerrero+ Rosing Legaspi-Guerrero+ Cynthia Guerrero

Top Right: 1953: L-R, around Nanay/Grandma Filomena Guerrero: Cynthia Guerrero+ Bong Yogore+ Hilda Elizes+ Jobo Elizes + Eleanor Gguerrero+ Minna Guerrero+ Bobby Elizes+ Eugene Yogore+ Cynthia Guerrero

Top Left: 1959: L-R: Bottom-Up: Mostly grandchildren

More Mix Pictures

Top Left: 1995: L-R: Maqui Licerio & daughter Taylor + Pinky Hollmann & daughter, Chloe at Licerio swimming pool in Orangeburg, NY.

Top Right: 2000: L-R: Laurie Licerio+ Norma Guerrero+ Christine Licerio

Mid Left: 1995: L-R: Chiqui Hollmann-Yulo+ Aya Guerrero-Valerio

Mid Right & Bottom Right: 1992: L-R: Chase, age 6+ Monique, 3+ Hans,2 + Mother Mimi. At Naomi Hollmann's swimming pool in San Juan, Rizal.

Bottom Left: 1995: Jocelyn (Joji) Guerrero-Acop+ Charlne Adelaide (Pinky) Hollmann

More Mix Pictures

Top Left: 1971: Nanay Filomena 73rd Bday at Mykonos Greek Restaurant: L-R: Merlie Elizes+ Beth Yogore+ Piding Guerrero+ Gene Guerrero+ Nanay Filomena+ Norma Guerrero+ Lulex Licerio + Bobby Elizes.

Top Right & Botom Left: 1980s: Fishing at the Creek at Gene & Piding property in upstate NY. Fishing group includes Norma Guerrero + Gene & Piding Guerrero+ Young kids Euric+ Gene-Gene+ Melissa+ Christina.

Bottom Right: 1984: L-R: Bottom-Up: Easter Sunday at Licerio Home: Ezsel Elizes+ Minna Magyawe+ Pinky Hollmann+ Mariefi Guerrero+ Christina Licrio+ Melissa Guerrero+ Euric Guerrero+ Gene-Gene Guerrero + Margot Guerrero+ Ester Elizes+ Marie Elizes+ Friend+ Maqui Licerio+ Piding Guerrero+ Friend+ Friend+ Friend+ Child+ Cora Elizes+ Jobo Elizes+ Bobby Elizes

More Mix Pictures

Top Pic: 5/25/1996: Mariefi-PJ Wedding: L-R: Lulex Licerio+ Ely Yogore+ Gene Guerrero+ Naomi Hollmann+ Norma Guerrero
Mid Pic: 1996: L-R: Lulex + Norma+ Naomi+ Ely. . .**Bottom Pic:** Atlantic City

More Mix Pictures

Pictorials & Captions

Mix Pictures: Group went to Atlantic City in 1996

Pictorials & Captions

Pictorials & Captions

1996 : Atlantic City Outing

1996: Atlantic City Outing

More Mix Pictures

Left, Top Right & Bottorm Right Photos: 1985: Maqui Licerio joined Miss Asia Pageant USA. She came out Third among the over hundred contestants. Another 2 contestants are shown.

Middle Right: 1981: Jan 6th Bday of Naomi Hollmann: Bottom-Up: L-R: Naomi Hollmann+ Nene Roxas-Guerrero+ Cora RamirezElizes+ Rosing Legaspi-Guerrero+ Susan Elizes-Ferrer. (Courtesy of Beauty makeup artist Chiqui Hollmann who made these ladies lovely to look at)

Mix Pictures during wedding of **Jun and Judy Licerio** in May 1998

Pictorials & Captions

More Mix Pictures

1994: During SerJr/Baba Wedding: All pictures show Naomi, Norma and Lulex taking care of Monique and Hans

More Mix Pictures

Top Left: 1992 Halloween USA: L-R: (Young kids) Chase Hollmann+ Yuri Valerio+ Hans H. Licerio+ Fima Guerrero Rada+ Raisa Valerio+ Monique H. Licerio

Top Right: 2003 Halloween USA: (Mixups) Noah as Batman+ Zachary as Green Lantern+ Taylor as Wonder Woman+ Monique as Beatup Football Player+ Riley as Baby Giraffe+ Lexie as Snow White+ Christina and Laurie as Mommy Giraffes.

Mid Left: Monique and Hans with dog Max, an Alaskan breed/

Mid Right: 1990s: Charlene (Pinky) wih her childen: Veronique and Chloe+ Chiqui Hollmann-Yulo with pamankins Monique and Hans.

Bottom Left: 1995: L-R: Young Licerio children: Monique+ Young Taylor-Marie+ Hans

Bottom Right: 1994: Hans Licerio, age4 + Taylor, age 1.5

Part 16
1989 Family Reunion in Pics

Our **First Guerrero Grand Family Reunion** was held in **July 4, 1989** in Rockland County, New York. The date was chosen because it coincided with the birth date **(July 5ᵗʰ)** of **Grand Matriarch, Filomena Jamito-Diaz Guerrero,** who died in 1985 in the Philipines, and this reunion was held in her memory. As this book is being created in 2011, more than 20 years have gone by, or almost 2 decades or one generation. I don't know if this reunion will ever be duplicated, but some mini-reunions of smaller groups have occurred since then through weddings of younger ones, birthday parties, despedidas, bienvenidas, graduations, and other milestone events. Of course, they could not compare with the big reunion event of 1989. Credit goes to my aunt, **Norma Diaz Guerrero,** who spearheaded the 1989 event and conducted hands-on management of the whole affair, from start to finish.

This souvenir book is now readily available and hopefully everyone will have a copy. You will be reminded all the time about the need for us to gather again in another grand reunion. I feel that some of you will clamor for it and volunteer to help organize this undertaking in the foreseeable future, hopefully, pretty soon, before the oldsters are gone.

I don't know who will volunteer as the the defacto leader or head volunteer. In fact I don't know if there is even a clamor to hold another one. But anybody, just anybody can also become leader. In fact, many members have good ideas how to organize another reunion. Of course, we shall not let only one person do the whole planning and all the work and activities to accomplish our goal. Many volunteers and asistants are needed.

Pictorials & Captions

The Day of The Guerrero Grand Family Reunion in July 4, 1989 was held at the home of Gene & Piding Guerrero in Monsey, Rockland County, NY

1989 Reunion: The food were brought by the family members. It was fun to watch everyone looking for food low in cholesterol, low in fat, low in calories and low in sugar. But it was hard to resist the opposites.

The young ladies played the Water Volley Ball Tournament with two team-opponents. One team is the "The Young" and the other one is "The Restless". **The Young members** were Christina Licerio, Kim Yogore, Tammy Yogore , Joy Ramirez, and Ely Yogore. The **Restless members** were Chiqui Hollmann-Yulo, Mary-Ellen Kimmeth, Leena Yogore, Beth Yogore-Kath and Mackie Licerio.

1989 Reunion Pics

1989 Reunion:

Top Photo: L-R: Leena Yogore+ Chiqui Hollmann-Yulo+ Beth Yogore Kath+ Mary Ellen Kimmeth+ Mackie Licerio+ Christina Licerio+ Ely Yogore+ Kim Yogore at back+ Joy Ramirez-hidden+ . . . .

Middle Photo: L-R: Leena Yogore+ Maqui Licerio+ Mary Ellen Kimmeth + Elizabeth Yogore+ Chiqui Yulo at back+ . . . .

Botom Photo: L-R: Joy Ramirez+ Ely Yogore + Christina Licerio+ Girl? + Kim Yogore at back.

1989 Reunion

Top Pic: L-R: 1Row: Gene-gene Guerrero+ Hilda Ramirez + MaryEllen Kimmeth+ Arcy Rada+ Bobby Elizes+ Chevy Elizes+. . . **2Row:** Aya Valerio+ BabyYuri Valerio+ Eszel Elizes+ Joy Magyawe+ Joy Ramirez+ Kim Yogore+. . . **3Row:** Piding Gurrero+ Zeny Guerrero+ BabyNoelle Bowen+ Tetchie Bowen+ Cora Elizes+ Christina Licerio+ Mackie Licerio+ Beth Yogore+ Laurie Licerio+ Merlie Elizes+ Lulex Licerio+ . . .**4Row:** VideoMan?+ Nonoy Yogore+ Chiqui Hollmann-Yulo+ Norma Guerrero+ Jun Licerio+ Michelle Yogore+ JohnPaul Magyawe+ Leena Yogore+ Ed Licerio

Bottom Pic: L-R: 1Row: Aya+ Eszel+ Johannah+ Joy+ Kim+ . . . **2Row:** Zeny+ Cora+ BabyNoelle+ Tetchie+ Christina+ Mackie+ Beth+ Laurie+ Lulex+ . . . **3Row:** Nonoy+ Chiqui+ Norma+ Jun+ Michelle+ JohnPaul+ Leena+ Ed+ Kim+ John

Pictorials & Captions

1989 Reunion Pics

Top Photo: L-R: Eliza (Ely) Guerrero Yogore + Dr. Mariano (Nonoy) Yogore Jr.

Left Photo: L-R: Baby Noelle Bowen, age 1+ Ester (Tetchie) Elizes Bowen+ Cora Ramirez Elizes+ Piding Guerrero

Right Photo: L-R: Kim Yogore+ Chiqui Hollmann Yulo+ Aya Guerrero Valerio + Eliza Guerrero Yogore

1989 Reunion Pics

The evening was spent on having sumptuous dinner at the Dynasty Inn, followed by dancing, playing games and group picture-taking.

Top Pic: L-R: 1Row: Eugene+ Oyie+ Eszel+ Guest+ Aya+ Chiqui+ Mackie+ Minna+ Melissa+ Joy+ Euric+ Gene-gene+ . . .**2Row:** Guest+ Merlie+ Tetchie+ Noelle+ MaryEllen+ Dylan+ Lulex+ Ely+ Piding+ Cora+ Norma+ . . .**3Row:** Kim+ Christina+ Michell+ Leena+ Bobby+ Guest+ Guest+ Kath+ Beth+ Guest+ Guy+ Jun+ Nonoy+ Ed+ Rico+ Hilda+ Chevy+ Joy+ Jackie+ (back) Kim+ John

Bottom Pic: Almost same caption

1989 Reunion Pics

1989 Reunion

Top Left: Chiqui Hollmann Yulo and Jun Licerio dancing the "whop"

Top Right: Laurie Licerio+ Jun Licerio+ John Yogore, doing the "musical chairs"

Bottom Left: More musical chairs game and dance.

Botom Right: Couple Rico Ramirez & Hilda Elizes Ramirez, doing the "last tango" under watchful eyes of Merlie Elizes, Peping Magyawe, Ed Licerio and others.

Part 17
Grandpa Guerrero Book - Ang Biblos

A man who studies theology in the Roman Catholic Church Seminary becomes a **Priest.** It is also the same in the Protestant Church. Young men finish their course in theology at the Seminary and becomes **Pastor or Minister.** Their academic subjects and topics of educational discussions are similar in many respects. They differ only in certain doctrines, practices and philisophy. Basically they are priests and pastors and cater to the religous life of the people and the community.

I want the younger generation in our family to understand that **Tatay Genio or Grandfather** is a man of the cloth or pastor or practitioner of priesthood just like the catholic priests. The major difference is that pastors are allowed to marry and raise families, while the priests are not. That being the case, we can conclude that Tatay is a shepherd of men, literally, as he teaches religion and influence people to follow the teachings of Christ.

Tatay wrote religious writings in his lifetime, after he earned his doctorate degree, and after practicing for almost 20 years as a pastor in Bicol. He was very proficient in Tagalog and used that language to write his books. Unfortunately only one book survived. These books were:

Unang Tomo or Tomo I - Ng Genius in Tagalog (this one survived)
Ikalawang Tomo or Tomo II - Ng Modernus in Tagalog (no print exsiting)
Ikatlong Tomo or Tomo III - Ng Kristus in Tagalog. (no print existing)

The first book, "Ang Biblos, Tomo I - Ng Genius" had been published and we have the original print-copy. I was informed that this book had been used as reference material at the Union

Theological Seminary because of his teachings, his faith in God and steady devotion to a basic moral code. I cannot fully confirm the validity of this information because the seminary school never answered our letters despite repeated inquiries. The two other books, Tomo II, Ng Modernus and Tomo III, Ng Kristus, were in manuscript-form but was gutted by fire in Tatay's temporary home in Pasay during his trips. I dont know if they were also printed.

One original print copy of "Ang Biblos, Tomo I" was in Uncle **Arte's** possesion previously. He was kind enough to have kept and protect the book until he lent it to for copying. The first two pages are missing but otherwise the 474 pages are still intact. At present, Uncle Gene is keeping the original book.

Going through Grandfather's book, I found it difficult to understand because it was written in deep Tagalog. One had to be proficient or understand the language to interpret the meanings intended. Aunt Ely, Uncle Gene, my cousin Marinella (Aya), and I read portions of the book and were asked to comment.

Jobo Guerrero Elizes Commentary, 2003:

"Ang Biblos" book is quite long, about 478 pages. It's written in Tagalog and hard to understand unless one is good in that language, specially the antiquated and deep words. The book was printed in 1929, but Grandpa Genio must have prepared his manuscripts many years before. One thing is sure. Rev. Dr. Guerrero or Pastor Genio is well-versed in religious education and philosophical thoughts. By reading his book, one will note that he had read practically all the classical authors from Plato, Aristotle and early medieval religious thinkers like Saint Augustine, St. Thomas Aquinas, and 18th century philosophers like Kant and Descartes, plus of course, the Holy Bible itself, being a student of theology. He mentioned all these famous thinkers in the preamble or foreword of the book. He finished doctorate in Divinity and he knew his vocation well.

I noted that his belief and faith in Jesus Christ has never waned, despite his having divorced himself from the formal and traditional religious organizations to which he belonged, during his later religious preaching before he died in 1945 at age 56.

He said clearly and unquivocably that Jesus teachings are supreme and cannot be equaled by any author, thinker, philosopher or any famous man or martyr. But Grandpa Genio is used to quote the words of other authors to bolster his arguments that God was working through them.

The books has many wonderful stories of goodness and values. One can only be patient in reading the whole book, specifically the histories, biographies, songs, poems, plays and drama formats. I presume hat he had used many of these stories in his Sunday sermons.

I picked some lessons on page 309, about "Ika Siyam Na Aklat ng Genius Dogmatikus, Pangkat 1, Ang Simulain: (a fews excerpts)

1. Magparaya kayo at magpadaya ang bawat isa sa inyo, sa ikapapayapa ng inyong kaaway. (Let your adversary cheat you. If this will give him peace, so be it.) My comment is this: Is this not the highest form of Christian attitude against somebody who cheats you? Have you ever allowed anybody to cheat you and allowed him/her not to repay it? It seems to me, this is very hard thing to do, but that is Christianity in its purest form.

2. Sapagkat ang pagpaparaya ay kaganapan ng kautusan ng Diyos sampu ng kalooban ni Kristo. (Leting your cheaters get off the hook is God's commandment, like forgive your enemies, which is a virtue taught by Christ.)

10. Sino man ibig na kayo's dayain ay padaya kayo, huwag kayong magalinglangan sa kanila, kundi bagkus kayo'y makisama sa wala mang pagbubulungkulan; (Whoever wants to cheat you, let him cheats you, without any complaint). This is almost like Christ

teaching that if somebody slaps your right cheek, give him your left cheek also.

There are many more unique and original lessons from his writings. One must read them to appreciate them. It would be tedious to mention all his stories and parables. One or 2 pages alone could occupy one's mind into thinking that Grandpa Genio is a very unique man, one of a kind, who is truly a servant of Christ. Try reading just one chapter and you will be amazed. Please analyze the deep meaning of his essays. But you need to know the Tagalog dialect.

Marinella (Aya) Guerrero Valerio commentary, 2003:

Regarding Grandpa Genio book and quotes:
1. Magparaya kayo at magpadaya ang bawat isat isa sa inyo sa ikakapayapa ng inyong buhay. (He means na magpasensya na tayo at magpatawad lagi kahit na madaya tayo to have peace in our lives.)

2. Sapagkat ang pagpaparaya ay ang kaganapan ng kautusan ng Diyos sampu ng kaloban ni Kristo. (Because God's ten commandments is summarized into 2 which is: To love God above all and to love your neighbor as yourself.)

10. Sino mang ibig na kayo's dayin ay padaya kayo, huwag kayong magalinlangan sa knila, kudi bagkus kayo'y makisama sa walang ano mang pagbubulungbulungan. (If someone hurts you or betrays you, just just let it go and forgive. Befriend them again and don't ever mention the past. There is a study about keeping hurts inside and not forgiving and since God did not create us to be bitter, nagiging bukol ito, mga hinanakit na ito sa katawan. Most cancer patients are bitter people who never let go and forgive. Bsides they are also God's children so istead of condemning them we should bring them closer to God and His salvation. We were all created equal by God so even bad people are his children but as Christ followers we are responsible to tell them the truth.)

Pictorials & Captions

11. Bigyan ninyong panahon and magdadaya, kilalanin ninyo sila na sila ang nagbigay sa inyo ng kapayapaan at kahinahunan ng inyong kaloban. (When we let go and let God, by forgiving, then we have peace because we don't have to carry the burden anymore. Sabi ni Lord that vengeance is His. Do you know that mas masakit ang ganti ng Diyos kaysa sa ganti ng tao. And forgiveness means that person owes you nothing, dahil lahat naman ng meron tayo ay blessing din galing sa Diyos, not because we are good but because of His grace. People who were hurt also hurt others. So what Grandpa Genio says about knowing the person who hurt you means to look his past and see why this person became like this. Abusers were also abused. A child bears the scars of childhood even up to old age, specially when they have not surrendered all their hurts to Jesus Christ.)

12. Sino mang napadaya ay may lubos na lakas ng loob. Upang makapagpigil sa kanyang puso, at ito ang may kapangyarihan ng kaisipan upang bumuti and sarili. (It means na you are brave when you forgive, dahil it's not easy. Out of he abundance of the heart the mouth speaks, we we have to guard our hearts and always. Don't ever let any hurt dwell in it and because of this we don't let the hurts rule our life and we become better person, not a bitter one.)

13. Walang taong pagkatapos na siya'y dinaya at makilala niya ay mgpapasalamat pa at tatawa ng walang ano mang sukal na budhi, kundi ang mga pinagkalooban ng kapayapaan at kahinahunan. (Same with 12, only people who forgive have peace in their life. We will have many disappoinments in life, but if we gather treasures in heaven and not on this earth, then nothing worldly will ever bother us. We only please an audience of one which is our Lord and Savior, Jesus Christ.)

14. Pumasok kayo sa simulating ito, at ang lahat ng tao'y kayo'y lalapitan, uutangan, uulukan, lolokohin, at pagtatawanan. Ngunit sa kabala nito'y kayo' magiging anak ng pagpapala at kapalaran sa araw ng bukas. (True, kapag giving ka lolokohin ka ng lahat but

the true children of God know better because in the midst of trials we have peace which the people of this world can never have. And because of the peace that people see in you they will be drawn to you and they will feel the presence of the most high God in your life. They will see the difference of who is blessed and not. Only Jesus can give us the peace that surpasses understanding.)

15. Magpaumanhin kayo sa lahat ng mangyayari at italaga ninyo sa Diyos and inyong puso, sa isang matalinong kaisipan at may mabuting pagkatao ng mga aral at karunungan ng Diyos. (Devote yourself in the Lord beause everything that happens in life is part of His greater plan for you which is to prosper you and not to harm you. Then you are able to do what you were created for and that is to be a witness.)

16. Ingatan ninyong kayo'y huwag mga mulala sa katarungan, kaalaman, at mga karunungan ng mga tao. Upang magawa ninyo and simulain ng ma pagpaparaya at pagpapadaya, sa inyong sariling pagkatawo at sariling pagkatuto. Ang matalinong pagpapasiya, ay siyang kaganapan ng pagpaparaya. (Sabi sa Bibile: We are in this world but we are not of the world. So the wisdom of man is but foolishness to God. Only when we understand the word of God which is the Bible, can we have true wisdom. Then we are able to easily forgive others, and we are able to see the bigger picture in God's plan for our life.)

Eliza (Ely) Guerrero Yogore Commentary, 2003:

In the Preface of Tatay Genio Book, one cannot ignore the great praise nd admiration which was accorded the great works, teachings, and sacrifices of Jesus Christ, as the author (Dr. Eugenio T. Guerrero) writes, cannot be surpassed or compared with any other being for His excellence and greatness.

Also mentioned worthily is the foremost Filipino hero, Dr. Jose Rizal, who gave his life for a great cause of freedom from oppression, tyranny and domination by a foreign power.

Pictorials & Captions

Contributions of famous great men from the beginning of time to the present are known to have shaped and changed concepts and philosophies of their own respective societies, yet have been considered important in the formulation and adaptation of such concepts to our own.

Because of the use of the original Tagalog language as used during this time, this gives the reader the advantage to fully understand and appreciate the full context of the author's intentions to convey his great message. The book mentions philosophies, concepts and teachings of great men that helped direct and shape the thinking of the present. Toward the end chapters, "The Revelation Part", the author uses the dream concept to make the presentation more meaningful to converge his ideas for clarity of thought in relation to the inended message.

Those are my own assessment and impressions of Tatay's book. - Ely

Eugenio (Gene) Diaz Guerrero, Jr Commentary, 2006:

Helping my father plant young coconut seedlings when I was about nine years old gave me a sense of accomplishment for my daily activities. Seeing the trees after fifty years of growth was seeing nature in real time.

To write about my father is to see him through his writings. To know more about the man is to read what messages he had left behind. In his book, Ang Biblos, he portrays his respect and recognition of all religions. For a man to think of the universality of all religions in the year 1929 shows his vision of the world where we are today. We can learn from lives and thoughts of great men, about the messages they laid down upon us that we may use them as guides in teaching family values to live in peace with one another. The right things we do from the beginning will bring forth the best of our expectations.

Pictorials & Captions

The most outstanding example portrayed in his book is Jesus ethical teachings, which are inspiring. However the messages coming from other religious teachings had shown relevance and values of their own. Make a time therefore to read his book that we can share with others the messages full of good moral lessons.

Would his vision in recognizing the universality of all religions an their teachings be the path to peace for all mankind? Tatay Genio is a man of vision whom we can always be proud of. - Gene

Part 18- Ancestral Home In Talisay

Guerrero Ancestral Home in Talisay, Cam.Norte, Philippines. Gene is shown above. (Note: Ancestral house had been demolished in 2006)

Part 19 - Guerrero Cemetery in Talisay

Pic 1 - Nanay Filomena Guerrero in black+ . . . .**Pics 2 & 3** - Norma Guerrero

Pictorials & Captions

Part 20 - Emong Guerrero Clan & Herrera/Olivarez Families

Geronimo (Emong)T. Guerrero is younger brother of **Tatay Eugenio T. Guerrero**

Top Left, 1910: Matriarch Aquilina (Inang) Tanyag Guerrero - Our paternal grandma.

Top Mid, 2000: Iluminada (Luming) Guerrero, daughter of Lolo Emong
Top Right, 1980s: Carlos (Carling) Guerero, son of Lolo Emog

Bottom Left: 2009: L-R: Bottom-up: Raul-Rolly Guerrero+ Emilia (Emy) Guerrero+ Rico Ramirez+ (at back) Jobo Guerrero Elizes+ Rico Guerrero
Mid & Bottom Right, 2 pics: 2009: Pura Guerrero Amante+ Elvira+ Edison

Pictorials & Captions

Emong Story

Lolo Emong was born in San Pedro, Laguna. He has no picture in this book. He married **Maciana (Cianang) Magana** from Talisay, just like his brother who got smitten by Talisay ladies. He raised two (2) children, Iluminada (Luming) and Carlos (Carling), whose pictures are included here.

Luming Guerrero married **Pacifico Nocon.** They raised 3 children.

Lumings's first child **Antonio Guerrero Nocon** married a certain **Violy.** Their children are unknown.

Lumings's second child, **Aida Guerrero Nocon** married **Feliciano Ramirez** and raised 2 children: **Federico and Fezaida Ramirez**. Aida & husband and Fezaida are residents of London, England.

Luming's third child is **Pura Guerrero** who married **Ernesto Amante** and produced 5 children, namely, **Elvira, Elisa, Eleanor, Emily and Edison.** Pura's family live in San Pedro, Laguna.

Carling Guerrero married **Amparo (Paring) Belchite** and they raised 7 children. Carling Guerrero was Vice-Mayor of San Pedro one time.

Carling's 1st child is **Raul or Rolly Guerrero** who married **Cecilia Ulanday** and raised 2 children, namely, **Madeline and Tricia May.**

Carling's 2nd child is **Emelia Guerrero,** who remained unmarried.

Carling's 3rd child is **Erlinda Guerrero** who married **Lito Reyes,** producing 3 children, **Rebecca, Evangeline and Noel.**

Carling's 4th child is **Edna Guerrero** who married **Reynaldo Guerzon,** producing 3 children, **Michael, Jeffer and michelle.**

Carling's 5th child is **Ester Guerrero**, who married **Benedicto Velarde** producing 4 children, **Bea, Benedict, Christine and Bernadette.**

Carling's 6th child is **Elma Guerrero** who married **Mario Snovio**, producing 2 children, **Marilyn and Jasmine.**

Carlings 7th child is **Rico Guerrero**, who remained unmarried.

Lolo Emong's family is a big clan. The family tree is included in our Guerrero Family Tree website, **http://www.guerrerotree.yolasite.com**

Herrera and Olivarez Families
of San Pedro Laguna

Is very very difficult to trace our Guerrero heritage of San Pedro Laguna. I tried to write Ate Luming and Kuya Carling but sadly, both of them have passed away, without my knowledge. It's understandable as they are my more senior cousins. I knew them very well as they stayed in Talisay during their youth before their family migrated to San Pedro.

1998 Visit to San Pedro: L-R: Seated: Ate Pacia Herrera+ Ate Felisa Herrera Olivarez+
Standing: Gene Guerrero+ Ely Guerrero Yogore+ Naomi Guerrero Hollmann+ Lulex Guerrero Licerio+ Norma Guerrero

Fortunately, the grandson of Ate Luming, named **Eric Nocon Ramirez** answered my recent letter and supplied the list of names of Lolo Emong clan, the extended relatives of the Herrera and Olivarez families, some of whose members are known and close to me and to some members of our own family.

Some of their names are worthwhile mentioning in this book. Later on, my nephew, webmaster **Jobo Guerrero Elizes** will include their listings in our our Guerrero Family Tree wedbsite.

We are familiar with **Leoncia (Lelang Onciang) Guerrero Herrera**, who had a brother, **Cipriano (Lolo Panong) Guerrero Herrera**. Leoncia remained unmarried. Cipriano had three children: **Jose Herrera, Bonifacia (Pacia) Herrera, and Felisa Herrera Olivarez.**

Cipriano Herrera had two sons, **Antonio (Tonying) and Pablo (Pabling) Herrera.**
Cipriano and wife were killed during the Japanese time, so Tonying and Pabling were informally adopted by their aunt, **Bonifacia (Pacia) Herrera**, who remained single. Pacia owned and ran a dry goods stall for mny years at San Pedro Central Public Market.

Felisa Herrera married Cipriano Olivarez of Barrio San Vicente of San Pedro, who was an entrepreneur and once Vice-Mayor of San Pedro. Felisa operated a big scale flower garden, raising the famous Sampaguita, as a business. She brought these flowers during her visit to our family in Manila on All Saints Day. The Olivaez children are: **Josefina (Pining), Andy, Valentin, Juan (Jun) Emma, and Lovegildo.**
Their family listing is included in our Guerrero Family Tree website.

Pining Olivarez, a nurse, married **a Lozada**, an engineer, and produced 3 children: **Reginald (Reggie), Edward and Anglino (Lino).** They live in San Pedro.

Andy Olivarez, a nurse, married **Subhash Sethi** and had 2 children: **Ravi Alexander & Andrea.** They live in Livonia, MI.

Valentin Olivarez married and one child is **Monette Olivarez-Regudo**. They live in San Pedro.
Jun Olivarez married **Lucy Moran** and had 3 children: **Katrina (Kay), Maria Alexandrea (Alex) and Maria Margarita.** They live in

Livonia, MI

Emma Olivarez Angeles had 4 children: **Edwin, Engel, Elmer, and Erlyn.**
Leovigildo (Leo/Lovi) Olivarez married and had a son, **Leovigildo Jr.** They are in Livonia, MI

Emong Guerrero + Herrera + Olivarez Pics

Top Left: 2008: L-R: Eric Nocon Ramirez+ Benedict (Toto) Guerrero Velarde
Top Right: 2008: L-R: Emelia (Emy) Guerrero + Jobo Guerrero Elizes

Mid Left: 2007: L-R: Eric Nocon Ramirez+ Daughter1+ Son+ Daughter2 with baby
Mid Right: 2007: L-R: Aida Nocon Ramirez + Feliciano Ramirez, both based in London

Bottom Left: 2009: Family Pic of Monette Olivarez Regudo+ Husband+ 3 children, based in San Pedro
Botom Right: 2007: Felaida Nocon Ramirez+ Mom Aida Ramirez, based in London

Part 21 - Juanso (Tata Ansoy) Diaz Clan+ Ramon Diaz + Inciang Diaz Fmilies

A: Ramon Diaz Family

Juanso Diaz or Tata Ansoy is older brother of our grandfather, **Florentino (Tata Tinong) Diaz.** Tata Ansoy is the father of our famous uncle, Tio Ramon Diaz, the Chief Steward of MV Don Julio of the Maritima Lines. Tio Ramon and my mother, Nanay Filo are first cousins and they were born more less in the same period of 1898-1900.

Diaz Family Picture during funeral of Juanso Diaz in Cebu, Circa 1930. The ages of the two children of Tio Ramon shown more less tell the year, as we dont know the date of death of Tata Ansoy. Young Ramon Jr and Ben were born in mid 1920s.
Caption: (1) In the casket is Juanso Diaz, or Tata Ansoy, born bout 1865 - died about 1930, age ab. 65.
Standing, L-R: (1) Unk Lady +(2) Tia Cianng, holding child Ramon Jr+ (3) Unk Gent + (4) Tio Ramon in white holding child Ben + (5) Unkn Gent holding child Remedios + (6) Unk Gent + (7) Unk Gent + (8) Nana Bitang, baby sitter/yaya + (9) Unk Lady in white blouse.

Juanso Diaz, also known as Tata Ansoy married to Casimira Ramirez, who was from the the Bicol province. They were blessed with a son, named Ramon, who we call Tio Ramon. Casimira died during birth of Ramon.

Tata Ansoy was widowed and hired a nanny, Nana Bita, to care for his son. When Tio Ramon was growing up, they decided decided to settle in Cebu. There Ramon finished schooling and was employed in an interisland ship, after graduation. Ramon married Cresenciana De Catalaina, a collegiala, from Bohol. They got married in Cebu. They were blessed with nine children, namely, Ramon Jr, Ben, Remedios, Teresita, Michael, Lourdes, Wilfredo, Juanito and Francisco.

Teresita or Tita mentioned to me that Tio Ramon has another son named Hildegardo Enigo, a lawyer and Dean of the College of Law at Ateneo de Davao.

Tio Ramon became the chief steward of MV Don Julio of the Maritimes Lines until his retirement in 1985. After he retired, Tio Ramon went to San Francisco and then to Canada to be near his children and grandchildren. In Canada, he stayed with Teresina (Tita) Diaz, my closest contact person from the Diaz clan.

Tita is married to Atty. Sesinando Romero, Nanding, from Ozamiz City, Misamis Ocidental. They have two daughters, Maricar and Marivic. Maricar is maried to Sergio Flechia. They live in Montreal, Canada. Marivic is married to David Arnold and they have a daughter named Tatiana. The Arnols reside in upstate New York.

B: The Family of Pilar Diaz and Blas Abcede -

Nana Pilar is a Diaz, older daughter of Tata Ansoy, when he was still single. Nana Pilar was married to **Blas Abcede** and they were blessed with 4 children. **One child is Maria or Meming. Another child is Treming, married to Heralcleo Gamelo, which begat**

Heralcleo or Herling, who became a dentist. Herling had 5 children, which are Mariese, Gilbert, Judy, Jean and Michael. Salud or Alud is another daughter of Nana Pilar. Nana Alud is our closest relative and confidant from their side. She was always around our house to attend to our needs like special food that we always miss. These bicol food are Tinomok. Also Guinataan sa Santol, Guinataan na isda, pili nuts . .yum, yum, yum. I understand that Ate Alud had hip surgery and due to complications, she died. Salud is one of the devoted teachers of Talisay Central School and was well loved and remembered, by co-teachers, pupils, both past and present. **Another son of Nana Pilar is Severino, or Kuya Binong. He fathered Estela, Elisa, Antonio, Edna and Alex. It seems to me Kuya Binong was the oldest as he died at age 99 in 2006.** I met him before he died. Note: Tata Blas Abcede is brother of my grandmother Susana Abcede-Elizes on my ather side. Whenver I visit Talisay, my only contacts with their Diaz family are Estela and Herling. I have not met the other descendants, specially the grandchildren.

C: The Family of Florencia and Adriano Desembrana - Nana Enciang and Tata Dano

Another Diaz cousins that Mom remained very closely related during her lifetime was the **Desembrana family** of Labo, Camarines Norte. **Florencia Espanol, or Nana Enciang,** is actually a Diaz, a daughter of Tata Ansoy, when he was still single. That makes Nana Enciang as first cousin of my Mother. Nana Enciang was married to **Adriano (Tata Dano) Desembrana**. Their union produced **five children, Jose or Kuya Peping, oldest+ Rubio, died young+ Ligaya, married Alfredo Ibanez = daughter, Rosemarie, married to John Barraza= child, Noeh and they live in LA. Fourth is Rosario, or Charito, or Ate Charing, married to Dionisio, or Johnny Gaudia = only daughter Melba, maried to Ariel Garcia = son, Marco. The fifth is Dan, married to Josefina Pangelinan, wih 2 children. Most of the Desembranas live around LA, California.**

Here are the pictures and captions of the Diaz Clan:

The Diaz Clan:
Top Row: L-R: (1) 1920: Ramon Diaz holding Ramon Jr & Baby Remy at back+ (2) 2000: Salud Diaz Abcede + (3) 2006:Melba Gaudia + (4) Dr. Christy Diaz Aparece-?+ . . .**Botom Row: L-R: 2008:(**1) Edna Abcede Timoner+ Mr. Timoner+ daugher Marifaye Timoner + . . .**1990:** (2) Norma Diaz Guerrero+ Charing Desembrana-Gaudia+ Fred Ibanez+ Ligaya Desembrana-Ibanez+ Dan Desembrana

More Diaz Pictures

Top Row: L-R: (1) **2006,** Severino Diaz Abcede, age 99+ Estela Abcede DeBelen+ (2) **1985,** Salud Diaz Abcede+ Naomi Diaz Guerrero+ Estela Abcede Debelen.

Middle Row: L-R: (1) **2000,** John Barraza+ Rosemarie Ibanez-Barraza+ Baby Noeh Barraza+ Ligaya Desembrana Ibanez+. . .**2006,** Charing Desembrana-Gaudia.

Bottom Row: L-R: 2000, Juanito Diaz+ Teresina (Tita) Diaz+ Francisco Diaz + (2) Juanito+ Teresita+ Wilfredo Diaz

Part 22 - Jamito Family Tree of Talisay

One of the biggest clans in Talisay is the **Jamito Clan.** The Jamito clan has a website at **http://www.jamitotree.webs.com,** created by me, Job (Jobo) Guerrero Elizes Jr. The site has a long list of members and descendants starting from their **Patriarch, Santiago Jamito and Matriarch, Jacoba Magana, born in 1820s.** They have produced almot 8 generations of Jamitos up to 21st century (almost 2 cenuries). Nana Mintang is pominent member of this clan. She was called "ponggola" or "abucay" by relatives, as form of affection. She was a granddaughter of the main Patriarch. We belong to the **Severino Jamito line of the family tree.** The Jamito family tree started with **SANTIAGO JAMITO and JACOBA MAGANA, who were blessed with six children, namely Froilan, Claro, Agata, Severino, Braulio and Ana.**

Great-Grandma or Nana Minting (Ruperta Jamito) is the fifth child of Severino and Apolinaria Barilla. She had sisters, namely **Rufina**; **Victoria,** (this is family of **Tata Domingo Abrina,** whose children are Naty Manly, Ernesto, Rosauro, Menardo, Henry, Flor and Romeo); **Juana** (was married, had no children, early widow, and lived with Nana Mintang family); **Margarita** (this is the family of Nana Ita, whose children were Esperidion, or Tata Pedion, Severino or Tata Beroy, and Felicisima, or Nana Sima; **Cresenciana** (the family of Nana Vicenta Varin, whose children included Alejandro, Juan, Ate Tianang Cootauco, Filomena Ramores, Rosita, Leon and Rafael). Nana's brothers, namely **Julian** (this is the family of Apolonia, or Nana Polon, and Emiliano (tata Emin) Mase, whose children were Paula, Filomeno, Maria, Jose, Pilar, Mario, Jesus, Loreto, Fernando and Nana's other brother was named **Mariano**.

It is also important to note that the Jamito clan honors the patron saint, the "**Nuestra Senora Del Rosario**" in the town of Talisay. When every one of the children had their own family, they decided to continue the prayes honoring the patron saint.

Pictorials & Captions

The prayer is observed on Saturday following the October 4th fiesta in Talisay. The children agreed that the property (parcel of rice fields) their parents left to them be used to meet the financial needs of the family who will handle the yearly Novena prayer. The occasion is religiously observed, with the mass attended by the members of the Jamito clan.

A prominent Jamito member, **Belen Aguilar Buan,** who lives in Talisay, was the main source of the listing of the members of the Jamito Family Tree that was used to create the website in the internet. Belen was my classmate in Talisay Elementary School and we graduated together in 1947. Then we moved on to high school in CNHS.

The internet is very useful in having the Tree available and easily accessible to all descendants. Corrections and additional information can be easily submitted to the webmaster at job_elizes@yahoo.com. The website is www.jamitotree.webs.com

Part 23 - About Talisay Town

I also would like to add a note about Talisay, the place where the Guerrero Family started, where the ancestors & children were born, raised and educated. Talisay is cuddled by the Pacific Ocean at the northeast of Camarines Norte along the municipality of Vinzons (formerly Indan). Labo is at the northwest and San Vicente at the southwest. The municipality of Daet is at the southeast. Talisay is one of twelve towns that comprise the province of Camarines Norte. The other towns are the capital town of Daet, Basud, Mercedes, San Vicente, Vinzons (Indan), Labo, Paracale, Panganiban, Capalonga, Lorenzo Ruiz and Sta Elena.

1980 Pic, when the town plaza was clear + good view of the St. Francis Church.

History indicates that long before the coming of the Spaniards, a village already existed at the place where the municipality now stands. In the latter part of the 16th century, a group of Spaniards from Camarines Sur, believed to be the early settlers headed by the conquistador, Juan de Salcedo, toured the place in search of gold.

While they were resting beneath the cool shade of the trees that grew abundantly along the riverbanks, they saw other people around. The soldiers asked in spanish and with the aid of hand movements, the name of the place. The natives, who did not understand the language, thought that the strangers were interested at the name of the trees and readily answered, "Talisay". This was the word that the soldiers recorded into their logbook and hence has been called Talisay since then. The Talisay San Jose Beach Resort is famous for swimming and surfing.

Part 24 - Guerrero Famiy Tree Listing

Father - Eugenio Tanyag Guerrero, 1888-1945
Mother - Filomena Diaz Guerrero, 1898-1985

Their children are as follows:

Code 1. ESTER (born in 1914,died 1945, age 31)
     No code - ELIZA (died 1918; age 2, infant death)
Code 2. ELER (died 1992, age 72)
Code 3. NAOMI (died 2001, age 79)
Code 4. ELISA
Code 5. SER (died 2001, age 76)
Code 6. ARTE (Died 2003, age 75)
Code 7. NORMA
Code 8. EUGENIO JR.
Code 9 LULEX
Code 10. VENCER (died 1988, age 50)
     No code - KERIEL (died 1939, age below 1)

Only 10 children survived to adulthood and married and had children and grandchildren. This family tree is confined to those ten. Eliza and Keriel were not assigned any code.

FAMILY TREE (5 Generations)
LEGEND (GUIDE TO READING THE CODES)
0. - Original Generation (no digit)
1. - 1st Generation - single digit
1.1. - 2nd Generation - 2 digits separated by dots
1.1.1.- 3rd Generation - 3 digist separated by dots
1.1.1.1. - 4th Generation - 4 digits separated by dots
1.1.1.1.1. - 5th Generation - 5 diits separated by dots
EXAMPLE 1: RACHEL JEAN SOLIDARIOS is Code 1.1.4.1.
4 digits mean she belongs to 4th generation
First digit 1 means 1st child of EUGENIO is ESTHER GUERRERO-ELIZES, 1.
Second digit 1 means 1st child of ESTHER is SUSAN ELIZES-FERRER, 1.1.
Third digit 4 means 4th child of SUSAN is ANA FERRER-SOLIDARIOS, 1.1.4.
Fourth digit 1 means st child of ANA is RACHEL JEAN SOLIDARIOS, 1.1.4.1.
EXAMPLE 2: JOHN EDWARD O'MALLEY is Code 8.1.1.
3 digits mean he belongs to 3rd generation
First digit 8. means 8th child of EUGENIO is EUGENIO(GENE) GUERRERO JR, 8.
Second digit 1. means 1st child of EUGENIO JR is MARIFI GUERRERO-O'MALLEY,8.1.
Third digit 1. means 1st child of MARIFI is JOHN EDWARD O'MALLEY, 8.1.1.

FAMILY TREE FOLOWS:

1st Branch - ESTHER DIAZ GUERRERO + JOB ABCEDE ELIZES SR.
----
1. **ESHER D. GUERRERO**, 1st child, b.3/7/15,Talisay-d.7/19/45 + **JOB ABCEDE ELIZES SR** b.11/12/10, Daet, d.3/11/93, LA.

Pictorials & Captions

1.1. **SUSANA G. ELIZES (SUSAN, SANIE),** b.4/23/33,Manila, + **ARSENIO FERRER JR,** b.1928, Makati, d.1971, Makati. - Vancouver
1.1.1. **EMMANUEL E. FERRER (NOEL),** b.1954, Makati, + **ESTHER TUBOG,** b.1957, - Manila
1.1.1.1. **JAY FERRER,** b.1982, Baiz. + **Wife = Baby** Manila
1.1.1.2. **ABRAHAM FERRER (ABE),** b.1984,Baiz. + **Wife = Baby** - Manila
1.1.1.3. **SARAH FERRER,** b.1986, Baiz. - Dubai
1.1.2. **MARIBEL E. FERRER,** b.1955, Makati, + **ROLY ABELLA,** b.1950, Cebu. - Seattle
1.1.3. **MARVIN E. FERRER,** b.1956, Makati, + **EDITHA GOMEZ (W1),** b.1963, Mindoro. + **BENG PANGANIBAN (W2),** b.1956, Batangas.- RP
1.1.3.1. **DARLENE G. FERRER (EDITH),** b.Oct.1978. - RP
1.1.3.1.1. **BABY DARLENE'S DAUGHTER**
1.1.3.2. **MARVIN G. FERRER Jr(Macho)(Edith),** b.Sep.1979. - NJ
1.1.3.3. **ADRIENNE P. FERRER (Beng),** b.1992 - RP
1.1.4. **ANA GRACE E. FERRER,** b.1958, Makati, + **LUIS SOLIDARIOS,** b.1957, Makati. - Vancouver
1.1.4.1. **RACHEL JEAN SOLIDARIOS,** b.1983, Canada + **Husband** - LA
1.1.4.2. **KIMBERLY ANN SOLIDARIOS,** b.1986, Canada - Vancouver
1.1.5. **CYNTHIA E. FERRER (CYN),** b.1960, Makati, + **SOLOMON ROXAS (SOL),** b.1956, Makati. - Vancouver
1.1.5.1. **SOLOMON ROXAS JR. (CALOY),** b.10/8/79, Makati + **CORNELETTE ROXAS.** Wedding: Apr.14,2004. - Vancouver
1.1.5.1.1. **MONETTE ROXAS,** b. July 2004 - Vancouver
1.1.5.1.2. **BABY GIRL2 ROXAS,** b2010 - Vancouver
1.1.5.2. **CHARLI MAGNE ROXAS (CHALOY),** b.10/29/88, Makati. - Vancouver
1.1.5.3. **CANDICE ROXAS (CANDY),** b.3/20/95, Canada.- Vancouver
1.1.6. **LEOGARDO E. FERRER (LEO),** b.1962, Makati, + **JOSEFINA CANLAS (JOSIE),** b.1962, Olongapo. - Vancouver
1.1.6.1. **SUSANA MARIE FERRER (SUSIE),** b.1992, Regina,- Vancouver
1.1.6.2. **AARON JOEL FERRER,** b.1994, Regina - Vancouver
1.1.7. **ROMAN E. FERRER,** b.1966, Makati, + **ADELINA FAJARDO (LYNN),** b.1965, Calamba. - Vancouver
1.1.7.1. **KATHLEEN MARIE FERRER,** b.1997, Canada - Vancouver
1.1.7.2. **MARK RYAN FERRER,** b.1999, Canada - Vancouver

1.2. **JOB GUERRERO ELIZES JR (JOBO),** b.8/5/34,Manila, + **CORAZON BAUTISTA RAMIREZ (CORA),** b.6/30/35, Imus - NY
1.2.1. **ESTER ELIZES BOWEN (TETCHIE),** b.10/24/60, Manila. Single mom - NY
1.2.1.1. **NOELLE-MARI E. BOWEN (NOWIE),** b.2/13/88, CA - NY
1.2.1.2. **JEB JEFFREY ELIZES,** b.10/6/92, NY - NY
1.2.2. **CHEVALIER R. ELIZES (CHEV),** b.3/21/62, Manila, + **ELIZABETH GOMEZ ESMERALDA (ABETH),** b.6/15/57, Tanjay - NY
1.2.2.1. **KARINES ESMERALDA ELIZES (KARIN),** b.5/20/83, Tanjay + **AUNG MRA,** b.1980, Burma - NY
1.2.2.2. **CHAD ESMERALDA ELIZES,** b.8/12/90, Brooklyn - NY

1.2.3. **MARINELA R. ELIZES (MARIE),** b.12/30/66, Manila, + **VINCENT G. REYES (BIMBO),** b.11/4/69, Manila.- RP
1.2.3.1. **MARJORIE ANN E. REYES (MARJO),** b.7/7/90, Manila.- RP
1.2.3.2. **MARVIN E. REYES,** b.5/31/93, Manila.- RP

Pictorials & Captions

1.2.3.3. **MARTY E. REYES,** b.11/24/99, Manila.- RP
1.3. **HILDA GUERRERO ELIZES,** b.7/19/39, Manila, + **FEDERICO L. RAMIREZ (RICO, FRED),** b.1940, Pangasinan - Suisuin City
1.3.1. **LEILA E. RAMIREZ,** b.1/1/66, Suisun, + **BRENT WONG,** b.1966?, LA.- USA
1.3.1.1. **JARON WONG,** b.2000, LA. -USA
1312. **MICAH NATHANIEL WONG,** b.2001, LA. - USA
1.3.2. **JAQUELINE E. RAMIREZ (JAQUI),** b.7/20/67, Suisun, + **ALAN CARAGAN,** b.1966? Vallejo? - USA
1.3.2.1. **JADEN CARAGAN,** b.2000, Fairfield.- USA
1.3.2.2. **KAYLEN CARAGAN,** b.2003,Fairfield.- USA
1.3.2.3. **NOLAN CARAGAN,** B2006, Fairfield - USA
1.3.3. **JOY ANNE E. RAMIREZ,** b.1/8/74, Suisun.+ **HUSBAND** - SF - USA
1.4. **ROBERTO G. ELIZES (BOBBY),** b9/16/43, S.Pedro, + **MERLIE CABALE,** b.1948, Pagsanjan. - NY
1.4.1. **ROMERL C. ELIZES,** b.1970, NY, **DELPERSIO (W1)** + **EVELYN CALI (W2),** b.1959, NY.- NJ
1.4.1.1. **CHRISTINA DELPERSIO,** b.1990, NY - NY
1.4.1.2. **ERIC ROBERT ELIZES,** b. March,2002,Brooklyn. -NJ
1.4.1.3. **GIRL ELIZES,** b2009, China - NJ
1.4.2. **ESZEL C. ELIZES,** b.1972, NY, + **JOSE TOBIAS (JOE),** b.1972, Manila.- NY
1.4.2.1. **EMMELINE JADE TOBIAS (EMMY),** b. 1/2001, NY.- NY
1.4.2.2. **JARED TOBIAS,** b.6/30/04,NY - NY
1.4.2.3. **ERIKA TOBIAS,** b2007, NY - NY

2nd Branch - ELER DIAZ GUERRERO + ROSA LEGASPI (ROSING).
----

2. **ELER D. GUERRERO,** b. 8/25/19, Talisay, d.1992, QC, + **ROSA LEGASPI (ROSING),** b.1916, Imus.- RP
2.1. **ELEANOR L. GUERRERO (NOR),** Manila, + **ABELARDO ATIENZA (ABEL),** b.1946? Naga, d.10/2001, QC - RP
2.1.1. **AMAR GUERRERO ATIENZA,** b.1974? QC, + **WIFE SA-ME,** b.- RP
2.1.1.1. **EARL ATIENZA,** b. QC - RP
2.1.1.2. **THEA ATIENZA,** b, QC - RP
2.1.1.3. **BABY BOY ATIENZA,** b, QC - RP
2.1.2. **JEMIMAH G. ATIENZA (MIMAH),** b.1974, QC - RP
2.1.3. **EXEL G. ATIENZA,** b.1976, QC, + **WIFE JING,** b. - RP
2.1.3.1. **IZEC ATIENZA,** b. - RP
2.1.3.2. **ETHAN ATIENZA,** b. - RP
2.1.3.3. **EXANNE LOIS ATIENZA,**b. - RP
2.1. **WELHELMINA GUERRERO (MINNA),** b.1948? QC, + **JOSE MAGYAWE (PEPING),** b.1948? Lucena. - NY
2.1.1. **JOHN PAUL G. MAGYAWE,** lst child of Minna & Peping, b.1972? NY. - NY
2.1.2. **JOHANNA JOY G. MAGYAWE,** 2nd child of Minna & Peping, b.1977? Manila. -NY
2.3. **CYNTHIA GUERRERO (CYN),** b1950, QC + **RAY GASPAR(RIP)** + **ERNIE SAYERS,** b.1936, Canada. - Canada
2.3.1. **SIDDHARA GASPAR (SID),** b.6/11/74, Manila. + **DAVID DUNCAN** - Canada
2.3.1.1. **DARA RAY DUNCAN,** b7/7/2006, Canada - Can.
2.3.2. **DEVINE GASPAR (DINO),** b.11/24/81, Manila - Canada
2.3.3. **LOVE GASPAR,** b.7/29/86, Edmonton. - Canada

2.4. **EUGENE GUERRERO**, b.1953, QC, d.1997, QC - (RIP)
2.5. **DAVID GUERRERO (DAVE)**, b.1958 QC, + WIFE MARY, b. - Antipolo
2.5.1. **DAVY INEZ GUERRERO**, b.1986, Manila.- Antipolo
2.5.2. **RICHARD DAVE GUERRERO**, b.1988, Manila.- Antipolo
2.5.3. **LESTER DAVE GUERRERO**, b.1990? Manila - Antipolo

3rd Branch - NAOMI D. GUERRERO + CHARLES B. HOLLMANN (CHARLIE)
----
3. **NAOMI D. GUERRERO**, b.1/6/22, Talisay, d.11/20/2001, Manila, + **CHARLES HOLLMANN (CHARLIE)**, b.1905? Bulacan, d.1976? Manila. (RIP)
3.1. **HELEN MARIE HOLLMANN (CHIQUI)**, b.1956 Manila, + **PRANDY YULO**, b.1956 Bacolod. - RP
3.1.1. **CHINO YULO**, b.1984? Manila.- RP
3.1.2. **CHIA YULO**, b.1986? Manila.-RP
3.2. **CHARLENE HOLLMANN (PINKY)**, b.1957 Manila + **DR. DOMINIQUE GIRARD (H1)**+ **DR. RAIMON CARTIER (H2)** - Montreal, Quebec,
3.2.1. **VERONIQUE GIRARD**, b.1987 Montreal.
3.2.2. **CHLOE VICTORIA CARTIER**, b.1992 NY- Montreal
3.3. **MIMI HOLLMANN**, Single Mom, b.1960 Manila - RP
3.3.1. **CHASE HOLLMANN**, b.1980 Manila, d.11/2001 (accidental death), Manila. (RIP)
3.3.2. **JAYJAY HOLLMANN**, b.1995 Manila.- RP

4th Branch - ELISA DIAZ GUERRERO (ELIE) + MARIANO GARCIA YOGORE JR (NONOY)
----
4. **ELISA D. GUERRERO (ELIE)**, b.1924? Talisay, + **DR. MARIANO GARCIA YOGORE JR.(NONOY)**, b.1922-d2009, Bacolod (RIP).-IL
4.1. **MARIANO G. YOGORE III (BONG)**, b.6/20/46, Manila, + **RITA PENAFLORIDA**, 1947? Pototan Iloilo.- IL
4.1.1. **MARIANO PHILIP YOGORE IV (PHILIP)**, b.10/23/76, Chicago.
4.1.2. **MARITA EMMIE YOGORE**, b.3/2/79, Alexandria VA. - NY
4.1.3. **ANNA MARIE YOGORE**, b.7/11/80, Harvey IL.
4.2. **EUGENE ELER YOGORE**, b.2/26/48, Manila, + **RIGOLINA CABONCE (LYNNA)**, b.1951? Narvacan, d.2001, Illinois (RIP) - IL
4.2.1. **MARA KRISTINA YOGORE**, b.1972, Manila.-IL
4.2.2. **LAARNI ELIZA YOGORE**, b.1977, Manila.-IL
4.3. **ELIZABETH LILLIAN YOGORE (LILIBETH)**, b.1950RP+ CHESTER KATH (DIV)-IL
4.3.1. **ELIZA RUTH KATH**, b.1992 Brighton.- IL
4.4. **MARILYN PATRICIA YOGORE**, b.1/29/52, Manila, + **GUY THOMPSON**, b.- IL
4.4.1. **KEEGAN THOMPSON**, b.1985, Brighton.- IL
4.4,2. **SYDNEY THOMPSON**, b.1986, Brighton.-IL
4.5. **MARY ELLEN YOGORE**, b.5/11/54, Manila, + **EDWARD KIMMETH**, b. - IL
4.5.1. **DYLAN KIMMETH**, b.1985, St. Louis MO. - IL
4.6. **JOHN PATRICK YOGORE**, b.10/28/62, Manila, + **TAMMY FESSLER (W1)** + **SHANNON (W2)**, - IL
4.6.1. **CONNER FESSLER YOGORE**, b.1990, Brighton IL
4.6.2. **MORGUN FESSLER YOGORE**, b.1991, Brighton, IL
4.6.3. **ALEXANDRA SHANNON YOGORE**, b.1998, Brighton IL.
4.7. **MICHELLE MONIQUE YOGORE**, b.8/9/66, Manila, + **WILLIAM RUSSEL JONES (RUSTY) (H1)**+ HUSBAND2 - IL

4.7.1. **EVAN CASSIDY JONES (CASSIE),** b.1995, Southland MI. - IL
4.7.2. **DARBY ELISE JONES**, b.1997, Westland MI - IL
4.7.3. **NEW BABY**, b2009 - IL

5th Branch - SER DIAZ GUERRERO + ZENAIDA HERRERA (ZENY)
----

5. **SER DIAZ GUERRERO**, b.1925, Talisay, d.12/26/01, Cavite, + **ZENAIDA HERRERA (ZENY)**, b.1930, Cavite. Home: Cavite City. - RP
5.1. **ALBERT GUERRERO**, Cavite, + **ANITA ESTOQUE (NITZ)**, b.1959, LaUnion - NJ
5.1.1. **MARK GUERRERO**, b.1979, Manila, + **ROSE ONG**, Alaminos Pang - NJ
5.1.1.1. **FRANCIS ONG GUERRERO**, b2010, NJ - NJ
5.1.2. **DIVINA ANDREA GUERRERO**, b1981, Manila - NJ
5.1.3. **SER ALBERT GUERRERO**, b1986, Manila - NJ
5.2. **EMILY GUERRERO**, b.1957, Cavite, + **GERRY SICAT**, b.1956, Cavite - Seatte WA
5.2.1. **KARINA SICAT**, b.1981, Cavite.- Seattle WA
5.2.2. **KARLO SICAT**, b.1983, Cavite.-Seattle WA
5.3. **FINOMENA GUERRERO (NINA)**, b.1961, Cavite, + **CEDRIC IVAN MERCADO (BONG)**, b.1961, Cavite - NY
5.4. **SER GUERRERO JR (SERGE)**, b.1965, Cavite, + **MARIA ELIAZO (BABA)**, b.1964, Manila. - NY
5.4.1. **MEG GUERRERO**, b.1996, NYC.- NY
5.4.2. **SEAN GUERRERO**, b.2000, NY - NY

6th Branch - ARTE DIAZ GUERRERO (ART) + PRISCILLA ROXAS (NENE)
----

6. **ARTE D. GUERRERO (ART)**, b.8/16/28 - d2003 (RIP), Talisay, + **PRISCILLA ROXAS (NENE)**, b.1932, Alaminos - RP
6.1. **JOCELYN GUERRERO (JOJI)**, b.1956, Manila, + **DENNIS ACOP**, b.1956, Baguio - RP
6.1.1. **JACQUELINE ACOP (JAQUI)**, b.1985, Manila - RP
6.1.2. **DENNIS JOSEPH ACOP (DEO)**, 2nd child of Joji & Dennis, b.1987, Manila - RP
6.1.3. **DAVID ACOP**, b.1989, Manila - RP
6.2. **MARINELLA GUERRERO (AYA)**, b.1957, Manila, + **DR. RENE VALEIO (BUDDY)**, b.1956, Manila - RP
6.2.1. **YURI VALERIO**, b.1986, Manila - RP
6.2.2. **RAISA-YELENA VALERIO**, b.1988, Manila - RP
6.2.3. **ANDREI VALERIO**, b.1996, Manila - RP
6.2.4. **STEPHANO VALERIO**, b.1998, Manila - RP
6.3. **MARGARITA GUERRERO (MARGOT)**, b.1959, Manila, + **ARCEO RADA (ARCY)**, b.1958, Manila - NJ
6.3.1. **FIONA MARIE RADA**, b.1988, NJ - NJ
6.3.2. **KARA-JEAN RADA**, b.1991, NJ - NJ
6.3.3. **MYLES RADA**, b.1992, NJ - NJ
6.4. **DR.ARTURO GUERRERO**, b.1961, Manila, + **CYNTHIA SERRANO (CINDY)**, b.1962, Manila - RP
6.4.1. **CORINA GUERRERO**, b.1988, Manila - RP
6.4.2. **CHYLA GUERRERO**, b.1990, Manila - RP
6.4.3. **GYRO GUERRERO**, b.1992, Manila - RP
6.4.4. **CATRIONA GUERRERO**, b.2002, Manila - RP

Pictorials & Captions

6.5. **DR. ARTEMIO GUERRERO (TEMY)**, b.1965, Manila, + **GEORGIA ARCEGA**, b.1965, Manila - RP
6.5.1. **MIGUEL GUERRERO**, b.1994, Manila - RP
6.5.2. **FRANCESCA GUERRERO**, b.1996, Manila - RP

7th Branch - NORMA DIAZ GUERRERO - No descendants

----

7. **NORMA D. GUERRERO**, b.1/22/31, Talisay - NY

8th Branch - EUGENIO DIAZ GUERRERO JR (GENE)+ FEDERICA VILORIA (PIDING) -

----

8. **EUGENIO D. GUERRERO JR.(GENE),** b. 6/2/34, Talisay, + **FEDERICA VILORIA (PIDING)**, b.3/5/38, Ilocos - RP
8.1. **MARIEFI GUERRERO (MAFI)**, b.1/11/71, NY, + **PATRICK JAMES O'MALLEY**, b.4/5/69, CT - CT
8.1.1. **JOHN EDWARD O'MALLEY**, b.12/10/97, CT - CT
8.1.2. **CONNOR PATRICK O'MALLEY**, b.11/8/99, CT.
8.1.3. **AIDAN JAMES O'MALLEY**, b.10/23/01, CT.
8.1.4. **McKENZIEC RAYNE O'MALLEY**, b.2003, CT.
8.2. **GENE GERRY GUERRERO**, b.3/28/74, NY.
8.3. **EURIC V. GUERRERO**, b.7/2/77, NY + **KRISTEN WARD**, b1977- NY
8.4. **MELISSA FEDERICA GUERRERO**, b.1/24/79, NY.

9th Branch - LULEX D. GUERRERO (LEX) + EDUARDO J> LICERIO (ED)ulex (Lex)

----

9. **LULEX D. GUERRERO (LEX)**, b.8/1/36, Talisay, + **EDUARDO J. LICERO (ED)**, b.1936, Marikina - NY
9.1. **MARIE CLAIRE LICERO (MACKIE)**, NY, + **CARMELO SORIANO**, b.1965, NY
9.1.1. **TAYLOR MARIE SORIANO**, b.1995, NY
9.1.2. **ZACHARY TYLER SORIANO**,b.1997,NY
9.1.3. **NOAH CHRISTIAN SORIANO**, b.1999, NYC.
9.2. **EDUARDO LICERIO JR (JUN)**, b.6/14/69, NY, + **JUDITH ESCALANTE**, b.1970, NY.
9.2.1. **LEXIE MADELINE LICERIO**, b.1998, NY
9.2.2. **JANELLE NICOLE LICERIO (TWIN1)**, b2004, NY
9.2.3. **SYDNEY CLAIRE LICERIO (TWIN2)**, b2004, NY
9.3. **LAURIE JOY LICERIO**, b.3/10/72, NY, + **ELDON F. HART III**, b.1/19/77, OK - VA
9.3.1. **RILEY EDWARD HART**, b.Dec.2002 - VA
9.3.2. **JACKSON FISHER HART**, b2005 - VA
9.3.3. **LILAH BLUE HART, b2007** - VA
9.4. **CHRISTINA LICERIO**, b1974, NY + **BRANDON CRUZ** - NY.
9.4.1. EVAN **MARTIN**, b5/7/05, NY - NY
9.5. **MONIQUE HOLLMANN LICERIO**, b.1988, Manila. Mimi's child. - NY
9.6. **HANS HOLLMANN LICERIO**, b.1990, Manila, Mimi's child. - RP

10th Branch - VENCER D. GUERRERO + VIOLETA MISSION (DIDI)

----

10. **VENCER D. GUERRERO**, b.1938, Talisay, d.1988, Talisay (RIP), + **VIOLETA MISSION (DIDI)**, b.1950, Mindoro - NJ
10.1. **MARIA THERESA GUERRERO (THESSA)**, b.1973, Talisay, + **MICHAEL ANGELO ALBA (MYK)**, b.1976, Pangasinan - NJ

10.1.1. **CHLOE ANGELIQUE ALBA (TRIPLET1),** b9/6/05, NJ - NJ
10.1.2. **RAFAELLA RAE ALBA (TRIPLET2)** b9/6/05, NJ - NJ
10.1.3. **DANICA MARIE ALBA (TRIPLET3),** b9/6/05, NJ - NJ
10.2. **MARIA FELIZA GUERRERO (BABA),** b.1975, Talisay, + **REX RIBANA (DIV.),**
b.1974 Manila - Melbourne AU
10.3. **MARIA FILOMENA GUERRERO (LALA),** b.1976, Talisay, + **RICARDO (RICKY)
CASTRO**, b.1975?, Manila - SF
10.3.1. **JERICHO-COCOY CASTRO**, b.2001, CA
10.3.2. JAZZLIN CASTRO, b2005, SF - CA
10.4. VENCER KRYSTIAN GUERRERO (BIMBI), b.1978, Talisay - RP
10.5. **JETHRO GUERRERO**, b1984 Talisay - RP

Note: Two (2) children, **Elisa Guerrero**, who came after Esther Guerrero, died at age 2, while **Keriel Guerrero**, who came after Vencer Guerrero, died as infant.

Part 25 - Emong Guerrero/ Herrera/ Olivarez Listing

GERONIMO TANYAG GUERRERO LINE (LOLO EMONG).
Lolo Emong is younger brother of Lolo Genio.

Code E for EMONG (Geronimo)

E. **GERONIMO (EMONG) TANYAG GUERRERO**, 1890Ss-1970s + **MARCIANA MAGANA**, 1890s-1970s. (RIP)

E1. ILUMINDA GUERRERO, 1918-2002 + PACIFICO NOCON, (RIP)

E1.1. **ANTONIO GUERRERO**, 1940s + **WIFE OF ANTONIO NOCON** -
E1.1.1. . . ETC. ANTONIO **CHILDREN** (NO DETAILS)
E1.2. **AIDA GUERRERO NOCON**, 1940s + **FELICIANO RAMIREZ,** 1940s - London UK
E1.2.1. **FEDERICO NOCON RAMIREZ (ERIC)**, b1965, **widower**. (Note that ERIC supplied all information about their family tree, thru Tia Norma Guerrero, by regular post, in early 2004). - S.Pedro, RP
E1.2.1.1. **DAUGHTER1 RAMIREZ**, b1990 - SPedro RP
E1.2.1.2. **DAUGHTER2 RAMIREZ**, b1992 -SPedro RP
E1.2.1.3.1. **Baby of DAUGHTE2 RAMIREZ**, b2008 - Spedro RP
E1.2.1.4. **SON RAMIREZ**, b2000 - Spedro RP
E1.2.2. **FELAIDA NOCON RAMIREZ**, 1970s - London UK
E1.3. **PURA GUERRERO NOCON**, 1940s + **ERNESTO AMANTE**, 1940s - Spedro RP
E1.3.1. **ELVIRA AMANTE**, b1960s - SPedro - RP
E1.3.2. **ELISA AMANTE**, b1960s - SPedro - RP
E1.3.3. **ELEANOR AMANTE**, b1970s - SPedro- RP
E1.3.4. **EMILY AMANTE**, b1970s - SPedro - RP
E1.3.5. **EDISON AMANTE**, B1980s - Spedro - RP

E2. CARLOS MAGANA GUERRERO, 1920-1980 + AMPARO BELCHITE, 1920-90. (RIP)

E2.1. **ROLLY B. GUERRERO**, 1940s + **CECILIA ULANDAY**, 1940s - SPedro - RP
E2.1.1. **MADELEINE U. GUERRERO**, 1970s - RP
E2.1.1.1. . .Etd . . MADELEINE **CHILDREN**.
E2.1.2. **TRICIA MAY U. GUERRERO**, 1970s -RP
E2.1.2.1. . . .Etc . .TRICIA **CHILDREN**.
E2.2. **EMELIA B. GUERRERO**, 1940s - SPedro - RP
E2.3. **ERLINDA B. GUERRERO**, 1950s + **LITO REYES**, 1950s - SPedro - RP
E2.3.1. **REBECCA GUERRERO REYES**, 1970s - RP
E2.3.2. **EVANGELINE GUERRERO REYES**, 1970s - RP
E2.3.3. **JOEL GUERRERO REYES**, 1970s - RP
E2.4. **EDNA B. GUERRERO,** 1950s (RIP)+ **REYNALDO GUERZON**, 1950s - Ilocos RP
E2.4.1. **MICHAEL GUERRERO GUERZON**, 1970s - Ilocos RP
E2.4.2. **JEFER GUERRERO GUERZON**, 1970s - Ilocos RP
E2.4.3. **MICHELLE GUERRERO GUERZON**, 1970s - Ilocos RP
E2.5. **ESTER B. GUERRERO**, 1950s (RIP) + **BENEDICTO VELARDE**, 1950s - SPedro RP

Pictorials & Captions

E2.5.1. BEA GUERRERO VELARDE, 1970s - SanPedro RP
E2.5.2. BENEDICT GUERRERO VELARDE (TOTO), 1970s - SanPedro RP
E2.5.3. CHRISTINE GUERRERO VELARDE, 1970s - SanPedro RP
E2.5.4. BERNADETE GUERRERO VELARDE, 1980s - SanPedro RP
E2.6. ELMA B. GUERRERO, 1950s + MARIO INOVIO - RP
E2.6.1. MARILYN GUERRERO INOVIO, 1970s - RP
E2.6.2. JASMIN GUERRERO INOVIO, 1970s - RP
E2.7. RICO B. GUERRERO, 1960s, single. - RP

HERRERA & OLIVAREZ Families of San pedro, Laguna

Code: H - HERRERA Family of San Pedro

H1. LEONCIA HERRERA (LELANG ONCIANG), unmarried, b.1880's, d.1950's, San Pedro, aunt of TIA PACIA & TIA FELISA. Tracing her blood kinship with LOLO GENIO GUERRERO is still difficult. Is her middle name Guerrero or Tanyag, we don't know yet? Still to be searched are San Pedro Register of Deeds, Bu.of Statistics, Church archives, and municipal cemetery. No children, being unmarried.

H2. CIPRIANO HERRERA, b1880s, Leoncia's brother, father of Jose, Pacia, & Felisa. (RIP)
H2.1. JOSE HERRERA, b1908, SPedro, d.1942 (killed by Japanese) + **WIFE HERRERA** - (BOTH RIP)
H2.1.1. ANTONIO HERRERA (TONYING), b.1932 (RIP)
H2.1.2. PABLO HERRERA (PABLING), b.1934 SPedro, d.1998,SPedro (RIP)
H2.1.3...etc...(Tonying & Pabling's Siblings - unknown).
H2.2. BONIFACIA HERRERA (TIA PACIA), b.1911,SPedro, d.1/19/2001, SPedro, unmarried - (RIP)
H2.3. FELISA HERRERA (TIA FELISA), b.1912,SPedro, d.6/19/2000, SPedro + **CIPRIANO OLIVAREZ (KA PANONG)**, b.1908, d.1980's, S.Pedro (RIP)
H2.3.1. JOSEFINA OLIVAREZ (PINING), b.1942 SPedro -d2000s (RIP) + **ENGR. LOZADA** b.1940 - RP
H2.3.1.1. REGINALDO LOZADA (REGGIE), b.1976, Spedro - RP
H2.3.1.2. EDWARD LOZADA, b.1978 Spedro - RP
H2.3.1.3. ANGELINO LOZADA (LINO), b.1980 Spedro - RP
H2.3.2. ANDY OLIVAREZ, b.1944 S.Pedro, d.12/3/99, Michigan,(RIP@54) + **SUBHASH SETHI**, b.1942 - MI
H2.3.2.1. RAVI ALEXANDER SETHI, b.1978 Michigan- MI
H2.3.2.2. ANDREA SETHI, b.1980 Michigan - MI
H2.3.3. VALENTIN OLIVAREZ, b.1946 S.Pedro, + WIFE OLIVAREZ, b.1947 - RP
H2.3.3.1. MONETTE OLIVAREZ, b.1974 SPedro, + **HUSBAND REGUDO**, b.1972 - S.PEDRO
H2.3.3.2. . . .MONETTE SIBLINGS...Etc No details

Pictorials & Captions

H2.3.4. **JUAN OLIVAREZ (JUN)**, b.1948 S.Pedro, + **LUCY ROMAN**, b.1949 RP - Livonia MI

H2.3.4.1. **KATRINE ROMAN OLIVAREZ (KAY),** b.1980 Phils - Livonia MI

H2.3.4.2. **MARIA ALEXANDRIA ROMAN OLIVAREZ (ALIX),** b.1981 Phils - Livonia MI

H2.3.4.3. **MARIMARGARITA ROMAN OLIVAREZ (M-M),** A b.1983 Phils - Livonia MI

H2.3.5. **EMMA OLIVAREZ**, b.1950 S.Pedro, + **HUSBAND ANGELES**, b.1949 Phils. - Augusta (Martinez) GA

H2.3.5.1. **EDWIN O. ANGELES**, b.1976 Phils - Augusta GA

H2.3.5.2. **ENGEL O. ANGELES**, b.1978 Phils + **WIFE OF ENGEL** - Augusta GA

H2.3.5.3. **ELMER O. ANGELES**, b.1980 Phils - Augusta GA

H2.3.5.4. **ERLYN O. ANGELES**, b.1982 Phils - Augusta GA

H2.3.6. **LEOVIGILDO OLIVAREZ (LOVIE OR LEO)**, b.1952 S.Pedro, + **WIFE OF LOVIE**, b.1953 Phils. - Livonia MI

H2.3.6.1. **LEOVIGILDO OLIVAREZ JR (WED)**, b.1978 Phils - Livonia MI

H2.3.6.2. **PAOLO OLIVAREZ (PA)**, b.1981 Phils - Livonia MI

H2.3.6.3. **ANYA OLIVAREZ**, b.1985 Phils - Livonia MI

H2.3.6.4. **PRIMO OLIVAREZ (EMOY),** b.1987 Phils - Livonia MI

OTHERS1. **ELISA GUERRERO**. She was a certain Guerrero, a seamstress, contemporary age of Tia Pacia & Tia Felisa, unmarried, stayed at Tia Pacia's house. The blood kinship to this Guerrero woman is not fully defined. Nobody has described her bloodline. She remained a good friend to Tia Pacia and the Herreras.

Part 26 - Juanso/ Ramon/ Pilar/ Inciang Diaz-Desembrana Listing

----

JUANSO DIAZ FAMILY TREE - Using Code D

D. **JUAN DIAZ, B1865-RIP + WIFE A, SURNAME?, B1866-RIP**

D1. **PILAR DIAZ, B1886-RIP + BLAS ABCEDE, B1885-RIP**

D1.1. **SEVERINO (BINONG) DIAZ ABCEDE, B1906-D2006 + WIFE SURNAME. MOSTLY BASED IN TALISAY AND DAET.**

D1.1.1. **ESTELA ABCEDE, B1930 + MANUEL DEBELEN. Home-Talisay**

D1.1.1.1. **CARLO DEBELEN, B1955+ VIRGINIA SURNAME**

D1.1.1.1. . .1/2/. . **CHILDREN**

D1.1.1.2. **DANNY DEBELEN, B1957 + WIFE**

D1.1.1.2. . .1/2/. . **CHILDREN**

D1.1.1.3. **CHRISTINE DEBELEN, B1959 + HUSBAND(EX). BASED IN CAROLINAS, USA.**

D1.1.1.4. **MARICAR DEBELEN, B1961 + HUSBAND SURNAME**

D1.1.1.4.1. **JOANNIS SURNAME, B1980S**

D1.1.1.4.2. **JINA SURNAME, B1980S**

D1.1.1.4.3. **JOAN SURNAME, B1980S**

D1.1.1.4.4. **JOVI SURNAME, B1990S**

D1.1.1.4.5. **EGAY SURNAME, B1990S**

D1.1.1.5. **RAMON DEBELEN, B1963 + JOCELYN SURNAME**

D1.1.1.5.1. **JOSHUA DEBELEN, B1980S**

D1.1.1.5.2. **JUSTINE DEBELEN, B1980S**

D1.1.1.5.3. **JASMINE DEBELEN, B1990S**

D1.1.2. **EDNA ABCEDE, B1950s + HUSBAND TIMONER. FAMILY BASED IN SWITZERLAND.**

D1.1.2.1. **MARIETTA FAYE TIMONER**

D1.1.2.2. **TIMONER SON1**

D1.1.2.3. **TIMONER SON2**

D1.2. **TRINIDAD DIAZ ABCEDE, B1908-D1950s + HERCULANO GAMELO, B1908-D1940S**

D1.2.1. **HERALCLEO (ERLING) ABCEDE GAMELO, B1930s + ELSA BUEN. BASED IN TALISAY.**

D1.2.1.1. ....**ERLING CHILDREN & GRANDCHILDREN**

D1.3. **SALUD DIAZ ABCEDE, B1910-D1990s, SINGLE. WELL-KNOWN TEACHER IN TALISAY**

D2. **JUAN DIAZ, B1865 + WIFE B ESPANOL, B1878. Home-Labo**

D2. **FLORENCIA ESPANOL DIAZ (NANA INCIANG), B1898 + DANO DESEMBRANA, B1897. BASED IN LABO CN.**

D2.1. **JOSE (PEPING) DIAZ DESEMBRANA, B1920, RIP + ROSARIO CAMARILLO. BASED IN LA, CA.**

D2.1.1. **BEN DESEMBRANA, B1942-D1994 + PHOEBE SURNAME, RIP. BASED IN LA,**

CA.
D2.1.1.1. **JEREL DESEMBRANA, B1960s**
D2.1.1.2. **DWAYNE DESEMBRANA, B1960s**
D2.1.2. **BOB DESEMBRANA, B1945 + CARLOTA (W1)+ GLORIA(W2). BASED IN LA, CA.**
D2.1.2.1. **RUBY DESEMBRANA, B1960s, CARLOTA'S**
D2.1.2.2. **JODEL DESEMBRANA, B1960s, CARLOTA'S**
D2.1.3. **ZENAIDA DESEMBRANA, B1958 + MIKE LIM. ZENY IS NURSE WHILE MIKE IS US NAVY MAN. BASED IN LA, CA.**
D2.1.3.1. **JENNIFER DESEMBRANA LIM, B1970s**
D2.2. **LIGAYA DIAZ DESEMBRANA, B1926 + FRED IBANEZ, B1924, RIP. BASED IN LA, CA.**
D2.2.1. **ROSEMARIE DESEMBRANA, B1960s + JUAN BARROZA**
D2.2.1.1. **NOEL D. BARROZA, AGE 1 IN 2006**
D2.3. **ROSARIO (CHARITO) DIAZ DESEMBRANA, B1929 + HUSBAND GAUDIA, RIP. BASED IN LA, CA.**
D2.3.1. **MABEL DESEMBRNA GAUDIA, B1950s + WOODY GARCIA**
D2.3.1.1. **MARCO GAUDEA GARCIA, B1994**
D2.4. **DAN DIAZ DESEMBRANA, B1930 + RUFINA PANGELINAN, B1930s. BASED IN LA , CA.**
D2.4.1. **MELVIN P. DESEMBRANA, B1960s + JENNIFER BRODETH**
D2.4.1.1. **JUSTIN DESEMBRANA, B1996**
D2.4.1.2. **JAN MIKE DESEMBRANA, STEPSON**
D2.4.2. **MIKE P. DESEMBRANA, B1960s + TRICIA (W1)+ STACY(W2)**
D2.4.2.1. **RYAN DESEMBRANA (TRICIA'S)**
D2.4.2.2. **ZACHARY DESEMBRANA (STACY'S)**
D2.4.2.3. **TAD DESEMBRANA (STACY'S)**

D3. **JUAN DIAZ, B1865-RIP + CASIMIRA RAMIREZ, B1880 (DIED AT CHILDBIRTH OF RAMON)**

D3. **RAMON DIAZ, B.08/14/01- D.11/10/83 + CRESENCIANA DECATALINA, B.06/09/09-D.05/20/79. BASED IN CEBU CITY.**
D3.1. **RAMON DIAZ JR, B.03/10/29-D.12/10/79, RIP + MARCELA PEPITO, B1929-RIP. NO CHILDREN. BASED IN CEBU CITY.**
D3.2. **BENITO DIAZ, B.05/06/31 + FELIPA COSITO, B1931. BENITO WAS ONE-TIME VICE-GOV. OF RAMON MAGSAYSAY, ZAMBOANGA DELSUR. BASED IN MINDANAO.**
D3.2.1. **ANNABELLE DIAZ, B1950S + HUSBAND NAME. BASED IN OROQUIETA, MIS. OCCIDENTAL.**
D3.2.1.1/2/3. . .**ANNABELLE CHILDREN (PLS LIST DOWN)**
D3.2.2. **BERNADINE DIAZ, B1950S + HUSBAND NAME. BASED IN CALGARY, ALBERTA, CANADA.**
D3.2.2.1/2/3. . . **BERNADINE CHILDREN (PLS LIST DOWN)**
D3.2.3. **CORDELL DIAZ, B1960S + WIFE NAME.**
D3.2.3.1/2/3. . .**CORDELL CHILDREN (PLS LIST DOWN)**
D3.2.4. **EDNA DIAZ, B1960S + HUSBAND NAME.**
D3.2.4.1/2/3. . .**EDNA CHILDREN (PLS LIST DOWN)**
D3.2.5. **DAISY DIAZ, B1960S + HUSBAND NAME.**
D3.2.5.1/2/3. . .**DAISY CHILDREN (PLS LIST DOWN)**
D3.2.6. **FREDERICK DIAZ, B1970S -RIP**

D3.3. **REMEDIOS (MEDING) DIAZ, B.12/18/32-RIP + ATTY. TEOFILO DONQUE, B1932. BASED IN CALGARY, ALBERTA, CANADA.**
D3.3.1. **FE ESPERANZA (PINKY) DONQUE, B1950S + STEVE EVANS, B1950S. BASED IN HAWAII, USA**
D3.3.1.1. **LEAH EVANS, B1980S**
D3.3.1.2. **SAM EVANS, B1980S**
D3.3.2. **RAMONILLO DONQUE, B1950S-RIP**
D3.3.3. **NAOMI DONQUE, B1950S + ARNEL BALTAZAR. BASED IN TORONTO, CANADA.**
D3.3.3.1. **ARJAY BALTAZAR, B1980S**
D3.3.3.2. **LISA BALTAZAR, B1980S**
D3.3.4. **LOUIE DONQUE, B1960S. SINGLE. LIVES IN CALGARY, CANADA**
D3.3.5. **ROY JOHN DONQUE, B1960S. SINGLE. LIVES IN CALGARY**
D3.3.6. **ELY DONQUE, B1970S. SINGLE. LIVES IN CALGARY**
D3.4. **TERESITA (TITA) DIAZ, B.10/16/33 + ATTY7. SESINANDO ROMERO, RIP. MONTREAL, CANADA**
D3.4.1. **MARIVIC ROMERO, B1960S + DAVID SURNAME. BASED IN FISHKILL, NY**
D3.4.1. . . **MARIVIC CHILDREN**
D3.4.2. **MARICAR ROMERO, B1960S + SERGIO SURNAME. BASED IN MONTREAL, CANADA**
D3.4.2.1. . . **MARICAR CHILDREN**
D3.5. **MICHAEL DIAZ, B.11/03/35 + CHRISTINE JOHNSON, B1935. BASED IN TORONTO, CANADA**
D3.5.1. **MICHAEL CHRISTOPHER DIAZ, B1960S**
D3.5.2. **CHRISTINE MICHELLE DIAZ, B1960S**
D3.5.3. **MARIA CRISENCIANA DIAZ, B1960S**
D3.6. **LOURDES DIAZ, B.10/1/37, RIP + ATTY. MATILDO APARECE. ATTY. APARECE IS RETIREE AND MANAGES THEIR FARM IN CAGAYAN DE ORO CITY.**
D3.6.1. **RAMON WINSTON DIAZ APARECE, B1960S + WIFE SURNAME. WINSTON CEBU MANAGER OF KL-BASED MGT CO. HE IS CIVIL ENGR.**
D3.6.1.1. **RAMON WINSTON CHILDREN**
D3.6.2. **DR. CHRISTY APARECE, B1960S + HUSBAND NAME. CHRISTY IS ONCOLOGIST. BASED IN CAGAYAN DE ORO CITY.**
D3.6.3. **ANGIE APARECE, B1970S + HUSBAND NAME. ANGIE IS NURSE, RECENTLY MIGRATED TO AMARILLO, TX. WORKS AS NURSE IN AMARILLO HOSPITAL.**
D3.6.3.1. **VIVO APARECE SURNAME, B1990S**
D3.6.4. **CARL APARECE, B1970S + WIFE SURNAME. CARL WORKS AS CHEF IN 5-STAR HOTEL IN MANILA.**
D3.6.4.1. **CARL CHILDREN**
D3.7. **WILFREDO DIAZ, B.08/21/39 + PERLA PADILLA. PERLA HAILS FROM HAGONOY BUACAN. FRED IS RETIRED. FAMILY BASED IN CARSON, CA .**
D3.7.1. **EARL DIAZ, B1970S + CATHY FABREGAS. CATHY HAILS FROM C. DE ORO CITY. FAMILY BASED IN CUPERTINO, CA.**
D3.7.1.1. **ELIJAH DIAZ, B1990S**
D3.7.1.2. **LOURDES DIAZ, B1990S**
D3.7.1.3. **NATHAN DIAZ, B1990S**
D3.7.2. **JENNIFER DIAZ, B1970S, SINGLE. LIVES WITH PARENTS AT CARSON, CA.**
D3.8. **JUANITO DIAZ, B.09/02/41 + ROSIE SURNAME. LIVES IN DIAZ ANCESTRAL HOME IN CEBU CITY.**
D3.8.1. **ROEL DIAZ, B1980S**

D3.8.2. **JENNY DIAZ, B1980S**
D3.9. **ATTY. HILDE INIGO (DIAZ)12/21/42. SINGLE. BASED IN DAVAO CITY.
FORMER DEAN, COLLEGE OF LAW, ATENEO DE DAVAO.**
D3.10. **FRANCISCO (FRANK) DIAZ, B.10/04/49 + NIMFA DE LEON. NIMFA HAILS
FROM PARANAQUE CITY. FAMILY BASED IN SAN FRISCO, CA.**
D3.10.1. **FRANCIS DIAZ, B1980S + WIFE SURNAME**
D3.10.1.1. **FRANCIS CHILDREN**

Notes:
More details are available from following Family Tree Websites in the internet:

www.jobelizes.webs.com/guerrerotree
www.diaztree.webs.com
www.jamitotree.webs.com

Contact: job_elizes@yahoo.com

Publisher - **Tatay Jobo Elizes Books** - **job_elizes@yahoo.com** - **tatay@usa.com**

Writings 1 Book, 2009

I. **Catch That Story** - *Tatay Jobo Elizes, publisher*
II. **Obit** - *Bambi Harper, Famous columnist*
III. **Speech, UP, 2003** - *Butch Jimenez, PLDT Executive*
IV. **Speech, Silliman U, 2006** - *Butch Jimenez, PLDT Executive*
V. **The Mission Moment** - *Dr. Phil Stack, Psyhologist*
VI. **Writing Underground** - *Mila D. Aguilar, Poet & Writer*
VII. **Academic Freedom** - *Mila Aguilar, Poet & Writer*
VIII. **Subanon Spirits of Rice & Land** - *Noel Cornel Alegre, Academician*
IX. **I Look Out The Window** - *Atty. Toto Causing, Lawyer, Journalist & Writer*
X. **Ride On A Bus, Poem** - *Anonymous via Melanie Ferrer, Budding Poet*
XI. **Why Am I Doing This** - *Susie Barbieri, Social Activist*
XII. **How To Court A Philipine Lady** - *Rodel Ramos & Jose Torres, Civic Leaders*
XIII. **Inspiring Young Filipino Entrepreneur** - *Lloyd Luna, Motivational Speaker*
XIV. **The Success Story of Ian Del Carmen** - *Lloyd Luna, Motivational Speaker*
XV. **Story of Bacna Surgical Mission** - *Sylvia Salvador, Civic Leader*
XVI. **1987 Philippine Constitution** - *Full Text (Special Feature)*
XVII. **Why Publish Writings** - *Tatay Jobo Elizes, Publisher*

Writings 2 Book, 2009

I. **Why Can't We Act Up Together** - *Susie Barbieri, Social Activist*
II. **I Know Where They Are All Going** - *Cesar Lumba, Writer & Poet*
III. **There Is Hope For The Philippines** - *Grace Padaca, Isabela Governor*
IV. **Pointers On Employment Abroad** - *Melanie Aquino, Dentist & Writer*
V. **Without KNCHS: (Love story)** - *Atty. Toto Causing, Jury Proponent, Writer*
VI. **422 Years Ago** - *Rodel Rodis, Writer & Political activist*
VII. **Filipino American History Month** - *Rodel Rodis, Writer & Political activist*
VIII. **Love is the Next Truth, poem** - *Daniel Rodis, son of Rodel*
IX. **A Need For Reflection - Gloom** - *Cesar Torres, Politial Activist, academician*
X. **Our Purpose Driven Life** - *Joey Concepcion, RFM Pres. & GoNegosyo activist*
XI. **Did Ninoy Die For Nothing** - *Joey Concepcion, RFM Head & GoNegosyo Activist*
XII. **Why The Filipino Voted** - *Pablito Lim, Zambales Businessman*
XIII. **Life And Love, Poem** - *Nannette Yatco, Dentist, Fine Artist, Poet*

Writings 3 Book, 2010

Writings 4 Book, 2010

Pictorials & Captions

VI. **A Plea** - *Miguel Reyes Reynaldo, Historian*
VII. **Int'l Youth Bowling, My Impressions** - *Marjorie Ann Elizes Reyes, Teenager*
VIII. **Mi Ultimo Adios (My Last Farewell)** - *Dr. Jose P. Rizal (Featured Poem)*
IX. **Aling Pagibig Sa Tinubuang Bayan** - *Gat. Andres Boniface (Featured Poem)*
X. **Rekonsilasyun Dula (Reunion in Heaven)** - *A Play By Irineo P. Goce (Kapule2 or Leonidas P. Agbayani), Writer and Playwright*
XI. **Forgery of Rizal Retraction** - *Irineo P. Goce (Kapule2 or Leonidas P. Agbayani)*
XII. **Maikling Kasaysayan Ng Malas Na Bayang Pilipinas** - *Ireneo P. Goce (Kapule2 or Leonidas P. Agbayani), Writer & Playwright*

Writings 5 Book - "Best Hopes" 2010 (About Presidebt Noynoy)
I. **The Challenge of a Hundred Days: Believing that Filipinos can...** - *Tony Meloto*
II. **The 2006 Ramon Magsaysay Award for Community Service** - *for Tony Meloto*
III. **Open Letter to Noynoy** - *F. Sionil Jose, famous writer/auhor*
IV. **A History of Pain** - *Juan L. Mercado, Journalist*
V. **An Open Letter to Noynoy** - *From OFWS*
VI. **Pursuit of Good Governance Advocacies** - *Marcelo Tecson, Financial Expert*
VII. **A Fervent Prayer for Peace** - *Cesar Torres, Academcian, UP Professor*
VIII. **A History of Betrayal** - *Perry Diaz, Columnist*
IX. **Corona's Thorny Crown** - *Perry Diaz. Columnist*
X. **Dawn of a New Era** - *Perry Diaz, Columnist*
XI. **Of Mice, Boys and Men** - *Philip S. Chua, MD*
XII. **A Hopeful Tomorrow - A Balikbayan Insight** - *Philip S. Chua, MD*
XIII. **Global Filipinos: A Sleeping Giant** - *Philip S. Chua, MD*
XIV. **Heart to Heart - Winds of Change** - *Philip S. Chua, MD*
XV. **Growing Old is a Privilege** - *Philip S. Chua, MD*
XVI. **Our Cruelty to Mother Earth** - *Philip S. Chua, MD*
XVII. **Advice to Grads: "Never Choose Your Heroes Lightly"** - *Ernie Delfin, writer*
XVIII. **Gawad Kalinga, A Progressive Movement** - *Ernie Delfin, writer*
XIX. **Why a Man Must Save and Invest** - *Ernie Delfin, writer*
XX. **Beautiful San Francisco, Pinoy Heaven** - *Ted Laguatan, lawyer, writer*
XXI. **The next President and PAMUSA** - *Frank Wenceslao, Pamusa President*
XXII. **Philippne Budget Deficit** - *Frank Weneslao, Pmus President*
XXIII. **Money Laundering: US Tools vs. Corruption** - *Frank Wenceslao, Pamusa*
XXIV. **Amid the Fighting, Clan Rules Maguindanao** - *Jaileen F. Jimeno, journalist*
XXV. **Why I Publish Writings** - *Tatay Jobo Elizes, POD Publisher*

Solo Authored Books:

Book A - **Turning Points - Empty Dreams** - *Job Elizes Sr,1968 (Reissue 2009)*
Book B - **Be Considerate - Behaviour Issues** - *Tatay Jobo Elizes (Jr), 2009*
Book C - **Piglets Unlimited - Wealth Untapped** - *Tatay Jobo Elizes, 2009*

Pictorials & Captions

Book D - **Out of the Misty Sea We Must** - *Cesar Lumba, writer, 2010*
Book E - **Fulfilled** - *Gloria & Miguel Reynaldo - Editor, Gonzales Reynaldo, 2010*
Book F - **Writings 7** - *My Vintage Pics* - *Tatay Jobo Elizes, 2010*
Book G - **Reflections** - *Life is a Journey* - *Bert Guiang, 2010*
Book H - **Writings 7 - My Vintage Pics** - *Tatay Jobo Elizes, 2010*
Book I - **May Bagwis Ang Pag-ibig** - *Percival C. Cruz, 2010*
Book J - **Letters To Matrimony** - *Irineo Perez Coce, Ka Pule2, 2011*
Book K - **Songs I Wish You Knew** - *Poems of Soledad R. Juan, 2011*
Book L - **Make My Day** - *Hilarion (Larry) Henares Jr., 2011 re-issue*

"Buy A Book or Gift Somebody"